ONCE SAVED, ALWAYS SAVED?

Posing the Question for Our *Eternal Salvation*

Catherine M. Vitetta

ISBN: 978-1-951280-50-5

Cover Design: Don Patton Creative

DEDICATION & ACKNOWLEDGMENTS

As always, it is with deep gratitude and love for my Lord and Savior, Christ Jesus, that I dedicate this book to Him. The concept of this book came directly from the Holy Spirit Himself, and it is only by His provision that this book was brought from its initial concept to full fruition. Please believe me when I say that I live the truth of John 15:5 every day of my life: Apart from Him, I can do nothing!

The Lord placed some very key people in my life who have supported and assisted me in fulfilling this writing task assigned to me by the Lord. I would like to thank Pastor Tom and Marcia Patterson for their love, support, and assistance in the writing of this book. I am particularly grateful for Pastor Tom's reminder that the judgement and justice of God always goes hand in hand with the love and mercy of God. I would also like to thank Pastor Dan Hudson for his love, support, and assistance with the completion of this book. Pastor Dan is always ready to answer my plethora of biblical questions asked of him 'on the fly,' and for this, I am extremely grateful!

Finally, I would like to thank Manifest International for their prayerfully considered assistance in the writing of this book. I greatly appreciate their skill at organizing the written materials, as well as their dedication to strictly adhering to the full word of God.

I am blessed beyond belief with the amazing Spirit filled people whom the Lord has placed in my life. To God be all the glory!

Contents

Introduction

For a professed Christian, there is nothing more important than our assurance of eternal salvation by the grace of God through faith in His only begotten Son, Christ Jesus. Romans 10:9-10 states, "If thou shall confess with thy mouth the Lord Jesus, and shall believe in thine heart that God hath raised Him from the dead, thou shalt be saved. For with the heart man believeth unto righteousness; and with the mouth confession is made unto salvation." As Christians, we long to spend all eternity with our Lord and Savior, Jesus. After we leave this earth, we yearn to hear these words from Him, "Welcome home! Well done, good and faithful servant." Just thinking about this incredible moment always brings tears of joy to my eyes!

Yet this beautiful scenario brings to mind the question of the validity of the doctrine called "*once saved, always saved.*" Of course, I would love for this doctrine to be true! Who wouldn't? Many people hang their hats on the assumption that we are all heaven bound for a really awesome eternity with the Lord once we come into the Christian faith, and that we have nothing else to be concerned about in this life in terms of where we will spend eternity. After all, we serve a loving God who paid the price for our sins. Why wouldn't we, who have been forgiven and are covered by the grace of God, wind

1

up in heaven after our physical death? After all, the bible says that God would have it that none be lost.

Many possess these beliefs after that initial moment of salvation. These people just seem to skip along in life assuming and believing their eternity in heaven is sealed with their new Lord and Savior without giving Him another thought. We need to know if this is true according to scripture. Our eternity is at stake!

The problem ensues when we cherry pick a few scriptures out of context from the bible that justify our personal opinions, or when we follow teachers and preachers who tell us what it is we want to hear. The bible places the responsibility of learning the true word of God on us! 2 Timothy 2:15 (paraphrased) tells us that we are to read and study the word of God for ourselves, and I believe Paul emphasizes this so that we are not deceived by false teachings which contradict the scriptures.

In my research, I found it very interesting that the doctrine of *once saved, always saved* was not at all presented in the early years of the church after Christ's death and resurrection from the dead. Rather, it emerged in the early 1500's during the reformation period.[1] The names Martin Luther and John Calvin are most commonly associated with the reformation. After his study of the bible in its original Greek and Hebrew languages, as well as studying the later Latin texts, John Calvin broke away from the works-based salvation taught by the Roman Catholic Church to adopt a belief in the doctrine that we are saved

---

[1] Sources: William J. Bouwsma who was fact checked by Encyclopedia Brittanica; and Believers Bible Commentary, 2nd edition by William MacDonald, edited by Art Farstad

by the grace of God through our faith in His only begotten Son, Jesus. This, of course, is true according to scripture, particularly as this doctrine originally included the belief that our obedience in living a holy life would be the outward proof of our salvation. Although these are truthful statements according to the scriptures, some who followed Calvinism eventually evolved their understanding of his teaching into a one-sided doctrine of God's immense love for humanity. In so doing, what became lacking in terms of a biblically based and balanced teaching was mention of the perfect judgment and justice of our God. God's perfect love also includes His perfect judgment. This can be seen in Psalm 89:14 which states, "Justice and judgment are the habitation of thy throne: mercy and truth shall go before thy face." Truly, we must study the love of God along with the judgment and justice of God in order to understand the complete picture.

I cannot imagine how horrific it would be for anyone who believes they are heaven bound to find out that their eternity will be spent apart from the Lord in hell on that day of final judgment.

> *Matthew 7:21-23 [Jesus speaking] "Not everyone that saith unto me, Lord, Lord, shall enter into the kingdom of heaven; but he that doeth the will of my Father which is in heaven. Many will say to me in that day, Lord, Lord, have we not prophesied in thy name? And in thy name have cast out devils? And in thy name done many wonderful works? And then I will profess unto them, I never knew you: depart from me, ye that work iniquity."*

3

I am certain that weeping and gnashing of teeth soon follow the hearing of these dreaded words!

There are only two known scenarios of biblically based eternal destinations for human beings, and they are heaven with the Lord or hell without the Lord. Eternity is a long, long time that we can barely fathom in this finite world within which we currently live. I believe that a study of the validity of the *once saved, always saved* doctrine within the context of the full Word of God is a very good use of our time here on earth. We certainly need to know if there is more to salvation than that moment when we said the 'sinner's prayer.' I can speak for myself when I say that there is nothing more important to me than where I will be spending eternity. As I previously stated, I long to hear these words from the Lord "Welcome home! Well done, good and faithful servant."

I would urge each and every one reading this book to prayerfully consider what you are reading. We serve a very gracious and loving God, who is also the perfect judge, who gives wisdom whenever we ask for it. James 1:5 states, "If any of you lack wisdom, let him ask of God, that giveth to all men liberally, and upbraideth (harshly criticize) not; and it shall be given him."

It is our Lord's desire that each one of us spend eternity with Him. However, it is the choices we make on earth and the heart attitudes with which we make these choices that will determine our eternal destination. For those of us who truly love the Lord, we should prayerfully examine what the Word of God has to say about this topic.

I love this anacronym for the word BIBLE: 'Basic Instructions Before Leaving Earth.' Thankfully, the Lord did not leave us 'orphaned'. He left us His Word in the Holy Bible which includes history, teachings and instructions! Praise the Lord for He is good!

Let's begin…

CHAPTER ONE

The Danger of *Once Saved,*
Always Saved Doctrine

Before we can even begin discussing the doctrine of *once saved, always saved*, we must first start at the beginning when the first sin of man was committed, in order to understand why the forgiveness of sin and salvation even became necessary. Therefore, we must begin in the garden of Eden when man was first created by God.

> *Genesis 1:1 - In the beginning God created the heaven and the earth.*

The scriptures following Genesis 1:1 denote the specifics of creation beginning with the creation of light. Afterwards, God created the firmament (heaven), waters, dry land (earth), all plant life, sun, moon, stars, and all the creatures of the sea, air, and land. Finally, God created man in His own image (Genesis 1:27).

> *Genesis 2:15-17 - And the LORD God took the man, and put him into the garden of Eden to dress it and to keep it. And the LORD God commanded the man, saying, Of every tree of the garden thou mayest freely eat: But of the tree of the knowledge of good and evil, thou shalt not eat of it: for in the day that thou eatest thereof thou shalt surely die.*

Shortly after giving this directive, God saw that it was not good for man to be alone. So, God made Adam a helpmate, a woman named Eve created from Adam's own rib. We might wonder why God even created man in the first place? Certainly, the scripture above states that one reason man was created was to have dominion over the garden of Eden and to tend to it. Genesis 1:28 states "And God blessed them, and God said unto them, 'Be fruitful, and multiply, and replenish the earth, and subdue it: and have dominion over the fish of the sea, and over the fowl of the air, and over every living thing that moveth upon the earth."

However, man was created for so much more than just tending the garden and procreation. John 15:14-16 states [Jesus speaking], "Ye are my friends, if ye do whatsoever I command you. Henceforth I call you not servants; for the servant knoweth not what his lord doeth: but I have called you friends; for all things that I have heard of my Father I have made known to you. Ye have not chosen me, but I have chosen you, and ordained you, that ye should go and bring forth fruit, and that your fruit should remain: that whatsoever ye shall ask of the Father in my name, He may give it to you."

Essentially, man was created to have a voluntary relationship with God. Nowhere in scripture does it say, or even imply, that we were created and placed here on the earth to serve ourselves, be happy, and give ourselves the glory. Our lives as Christians should glorify God.

We know that God gave man free will to choose to love and obey Him, or not: To choose between good and evil.

Some might ask why God would give us the ability to choose? Possibly, He gave man the ability to choose because true love cannot be forced upon someone. In order for love to be true and genuine, it must be of our own volition or choosing. Therefore, man had to be given something from which to choose. There was only one rule in the garden of Eden given to man to follow. That rule was to not eat the fruit of the tree of the knowledge of good and evil. That was it!

We know the ensuing story. The serpent manipulated Eve into disobeying God and eating of the fruit of the tree of the knowledge of good and evil. Then, Adam also ate of the same fruit. In that moment of the first sin or disobedience to God, mankind died spiritually and was disconnected from God. It was sin that separated us from God. God is holy and pure and cannot be in the presence of sin. As a result, Adam and Eve were evicted from the garden of Eden as well as from direct fellowship with God.

Thankfully God, in His abundant mercy, had a plan to reconcile us back to Him. That plan involved the future suffering, death by crucifixion, and resurrection from the dead of His only begotten Son, Jesus. Christ Jesus was the only perfect sacrifice or payment acceptable to God for the forgiveness of our sins. However, in order to be reconciled back to God, we need to believe this with our heart and confess it with our mouth and be filled with the Holy Spirit of the living God. This is called salvation by the grace of God through faith in His Son, Christ Jesus! It is only through our salvation that we can have the assurance of eternal life spent with God.

The question that arises is, after that moment we confess

Christ Jesus as our Lord and Savior, are there any further expectations placed upon us by the Lord? Are we forever saved and heaven-bound regardless of any future choices we make or declarations we claim, including those choices considered anti-Christ? Can we intentionally and knowingly change our minds and choose to reject Christ Jesus and His sacrifice on the cross after we believe Jesus, yet still spend eternity with the Lord? Once we profess Jesus as Lord, can we continue to intentionally and knowingly live a self-centered life of sin and disobedience to the Lord and still inherit eternal life with God? In other words, according to the scriptures, are there any specific requirements or expectations from God we must fulfill in order to remain in the faith after that moment we confess Jesus as our Lord and Savior?

Biblically correct answers to these questions are crucial for those of us who want to ensure to the best of our abilities and knowledge that we spend eternity with our Lord and Savior, Christ Jesus.

This leads me to the true danger of the doctrine of *once saved, always saved*. There are those who believe in this doctrine and use it as a license to intentionally continue in known sin. Such people use it to say that God has covered all their sin including their future sins, and they will automatically be forgiven regardless of their heart attitudes and the behaviors they choose to participate in during this life. Ergo, they incorrectly believe that this makes continued sinning in this life acceptable and of no negative eternal consequence. Many refer to this version of *once saved, always saved* as the doctrine of 'hyper-grace.'

I cannot fathom how anyone can actually believe this. *If* sin were acceptable to God, there would have been no need for God to send His only begotten Son to this earth to suffer horrifically and die in order for us to be forgiven of our sins! God would have simply winked at Adam and Eve if this were true, and Adam and Eve would still be living in the Garden of Eden walking and talking with God.

Scripture clearly states that sin separates people from a holy God! (Isaiah 59:2; Romans 6:23; Exodus 32:33.) God, in His infinite love and mercy, gives us the ability to repent of our sins through His gift of the Holy Spirit. We must work in cooperation with the Holy Spirit who now resides within us once we believe that Jesus is Lord. We cannot do God's part, and He will not do our part. Again, our relationship with God on this earth is a partnership. We must choose to live for Him in order to remain in Him and spend eternity with Him. Our free will to choose is never taken away.

But the greatest danger to the doctrine of *once saved, always saved* is the incorrect assumption that a genuine believer in Christ who professes to be saved but has a heart attitude which permits or encourages continuation in a life of known, intentional, and unrepentant sin is *always* saved and heaven bound! It breaks my heart to think that such a person, who genuinely believes that they are saved, will hear these words from the Lord when they meet face to face, "Depart from me for I never knew you!" Wailing and gnashing of teeth will be soon to follow. Please, don't let that be you.

My prayer for the readers of this book is that you will

earnestly seek the Lord in prayer and repent of any sin or poor heart attitude the Holy Spirit makes known to you. We serve a very gracious, loving, and longsuffering God whose desire is that none be lost. Truly, there is nothing more important than loving and serving the Lord and spending all eternity with Him!

Chapter Two

Scriptures Utilized to Justify the Doctrine of
Once Saved, Always Saved

> *John 3:16 - [Jesus speaking], "For God so loved the world, that He gave His only begotten Son, that whosoever believeth in Him should not perish, but have everlasting life."*

What beautiful words these are! For those of us who believe that Jesus was God's only begotten Son, who was the only perfect sacrifice for the forgiveness of our sins, who died a horrible death on the cross that we sinful humans deserved, and was resurrected from the dead three days later, will have everlasting life with God for all eternity after our physical deaths here on earth. The point here is that eternal life spent with God is ***only*** for those who choose the light of salvation through Christ Jesus over the darkness of their own sin. That is a promise from almighty God!

Again, we are given free will to choose between good/God and evil/self/the world. In fact, because we serve a most merciful God, if someone chooses to genuinely embrace Christ with a truly repentant heart on their deathbed after a life of selfish and sinful living, they can be saved in those last moments of life here on earth and spend eternity with God. When we stand before Jesus in the day of judgment, our eternity will be decided by the choices we made in this life and the heart attitude with which we made those choices.

This scripture obviously states that those who believe in Jesus will have eternal life with Him. What this scripture does not address is whether or not someone can lose their salvation through future choices *if* their future choices are made in opposition to Christ Jesus and His word without repentance before the end of their earthly life. If we are able to choose Jesus as Lord and Savior in the very last seconds of our physical life here on earth, why wouldn't we also be able to choose otherwise at the end of our physical life if we so desire? Free will should be able to go both ways if it is truly free, meaning unrestricted.

~

John 5:23-24 - [Jesus speaking], "That all men should honour the Son, even as they honuor the Father. He that honoureth not the Son honoureth not the Father which has sent Him. Verily, verily, I say unto you, he that heareth my word, and believeth on Him who sent Me, hath everlasting life, and shall not come into condemnation; but is passed from death unto life."

What Jesus is conveying here is that those who believe on Him and His work on the cross, also believe in the Father who sent Him. By the grace of God through faith in Christ Jesus, the scriptures indicate that such people **can** overcome the bondages of sin and death and would no longer be condemned. (See 1 John 1:9; Acts 3:19; Proverbs 28:13.) Such people will have everlasting life spent with the Lord for all eternity.

13

Conversely, those who reject Christ Jesus also reject the Father who sent Him. Such people who willingly reject the Lord *will* remain in bondage to sin and the wages of sin, which is death. These people are already condemned. Their eternal fate separated from God in eternal perdition is already set should they physically die in their unrepentant sin.

These verses make it very clear that only those who believe in Christ Jesus will inherit eternal life. However, we need to make note that nowhere do these verses address whether or not it is possible to renounce and walk away from Christ after having an initial salvation experience. And, *if it is* possible to renounce and walk away from the Lord after being saved *and* one knowingly, willingly chooses to do so, what effect, if any, would that have on their eternal fate?

~

Romans 10:9-10 - That if thou shalt confess with thy mouth the Lord Jesus, and shalt believe in thine heart that God hath raised Him from the dead, thou shalt be saved. For with the heart man believeth unto righteousness; and with the mouth confession is made unto salvation.

Again, we are saved by the grace of God through faith in Christ Jesus and what He did for us on the cross. We cannot earn salvation through good works of the flesh. Salvation is a gift *available* to everyone and given *only* to those who choose to believe in Christ Jesus!

Proponents of the doctrine of *once saved, always saved* use this scripture to conclude that faith in Christ Jesus along with a verbal profession of that faith assures a person of their salvation for all time. They believe that their salvation is now a 'done deal' so to speak, and their eternity with the Lord is set in concrete, regardless of any future choices made or heart attitudes developed. But we must ask if this assumption is true according to *all* the scriptures. The correct and complete biblical answer to this question is vital to understand in terms of where we will spend eternity! The very last thing any of us should want to do is make an incorrect or incomplete assumption regarding our eternal destination.

When I read this scripture, it appears to me that belief in Christ Jesus along with a verbal confession of our newfound faith is the starting point from which we are considered saved. As I read the holy word of God in the bible, there is so much that happens in us and through us after that initial point of salvation when we cooperate with the work of the Holy Spirit who now resides within us. Once we profess Christ Jesus as our Lord and Savior, the scriptures are quite clear that we must *continue* to walk with the Lord, and what that walk should look like. Proponents on either side of the *once saved, always saved* debate can certainly agree on that.

~

1 John 5:11-13 - And this is the record, that God hath given to us eternal life, and this life is in His Son. He that hath the Son hath life; he that hath not the Son of God hath not life. These things I have written unto you that believe on the name of the Son of God; that ye may know that ye have eternal life, and that ye may believe on the name of the Son of God.

Eternal life only comes by the grace of God through faith in God's only begotten Son, Christ Jesus, as He is the author and purchaser! Only those who accept God's testimony, and believe in and follow His Son, Jesus, are saved and promised eternal life. The bible is very clear as to what must happen within us in order to **obtain** salvation.

The question that arises and begs to be answered is are there any biblical requirements to **maintain our** salvation after we have an initial salvation experience? Is this something we even need to consider? These scriptures do not address this issue. Yet, it is vital that we understand the whole picture, so to speak, delineated in **all** the scriptures in order to understand the truth in God's holy word. Our eternity is at stake!

~

> *Ephesians 1:13-14 In whom ye also trusted, after that ye heard the word of truth, the gospel of your salvation: In whom also after that ye believed, ye were sealed with the Holy Spirit of promise, which is the earnest of our inheritance until the redemption of the purchased possession, unto the praise of His glory.*

The indwelling of the Holy Spirit, a.k.a. salvation, is promised to those with faith and trust in Christ Jesus. Once we confess Jesus as our Lord and Savior and are filled with the Holy Spirit, we then have the power to become a child of God. (John 1:12.) The indwelling of the Holy Spirit is our seal that we belong to God's heavenly family now.

During the time when Jesus walked the earth, it was customary to place a seal on your purchased merchandise so that it could not be mixed up with the purchases of another person and could easily be identified as 'yours only.'. The indwelling of the Holy Spirit is our seal!

We know that once we come to believe on Christ Jesus, we must invite the Holy Spirit into our heart to be our Lord and Savior. Certainly, when we claim that He is Lord over our life, it implies our ensuing obedience to Him.

The question that now arises is, if we can choose to invite Christ Jesus into our heart to be our Lord and Savior, is it *possible* to intentionally renounce Him at a future time and ask that He leave so we can return to 'being our own god' and doing what we want, when we want, the way we want? We can certainly view known, purposed, and practiced sin, after we have received salvation and knowledge through Christ, to be an intentional renouncement of our faith in, love for, and obedience to Christ Jesus and His teachings.

The concept of free will to choose implies that the answer to the question of whether or not we can renounce our faith in Christ Jesus after we have received salvation could be, "yes." Nowhere in the bible have I read that our free will to choose is taken away once we are initially saved. If our ability to choose differently were taken away after that initial moment of salvation, wouldn't this imply we are now forever 'prisoners' of God?

~

Romans 6:23 - For the wages of sin is death; but

> *the gift of God is eternal life through Christ*
> *Jesus our Lord.*

Everyone is appointed to physically die once. The verse that the wages of sin is death actually refers to the second death of everlasting perdition (punishment; damnation) for those who reject Christ Jesus. Eternal life with the Lord is granted to those who believed in Him during their natural life.

The question that arises is, can we maintain our salvation and eternal destiny with God should we decide to reject Christ and/or knowingly and willfully purpose to choose sin over righteousness? Many refer to this as someone who falls away from the faith in known, willful apostasy. The fact that the New Testament speaks about those who fall away from the faith and the apostate Christian would lead one to believe that these are, in fact, definite possibilities.

The proponents of the *once saved, always saved* doctrine would say that the apostate Christian was never really saved to begin with. Although this may certainly be true in many instances, we cannot make this assumption that it is true in **all** such situations because as fallible human beings, we are not able to correctly know or judge the true intentions of the heart in another person. Correctly judging the heart is something only God can do!

~

> *1 John 1:9 - If we confess our sins, He is faithful*
> *and just to forgive us our sins, and to cleanse us*
> *from all unrighteousness.*

When a follower of Christ Jesus falls into sin, the Holy

Spirit will be quick to convict us, and we should be quick to repent. True repentance involves us humbling ourselves before our Lord and Savior by admitting our sin to Him and asking for His forgiveness. It also involves changing our mind and heart so that they become aligned with the mind and heart of God, which changes our behavior. This ultimately results in no longer participating in the sin of which we have repented. Additionally, when the Holy Spirit convicts us of sin, it will grieve the heart of a true believer, and a true believer will purpose to fully repent in order to restore their right standing with God.

Since we are fallible human beings, often times there is a time lag between when our heart's desire became to be fully obedient to the Lord, verses when our behavior fully changed. As humans, we do and will make mistakes which sometimes involves backsliding into sin. It is in these instances that the intentions and attitudes of our heart become critical. There is a huge difference between someone whose heart is grieved over their lack of success in overcoming a particular sin, verses the person who decides they love the sin more than the Lord and knowingly, intentionally continues in that sin. The Lord shows great mercy and longsuffering with his children whose heart is to be obedient to Him while they are struggling in their flesh to overcome a particular sin.

When we come to faith in Christ Jesus, we essentially trade our sin for the righteousness of Christ. 2 Corinthians 5:21 states, "For He hath made Him to be sin for us, who knew no sin; that we might be made the righteousness of God in Him."

Now we need to ask: What happens if a believer chooses to continue in known sin intentionally after receiving our new state of righteousness through faith in Christ? When a professed Christian purposes to continue in known and intentional sin, their heart will become hardened over time to the point where they will no longer hear from the Holy Spirit and no longer feel any shame or remorse for their sinful behavior. Their conscience will be seared. This is a dangerous place to be in terms of our eternal destiny!

Matthew 6:24 states [Jesus speaking], "No man can serve two masters: for either he will hate the one, and love the other; or else he will hold to the one, and despise the other. Ye cannot serve God and mammon." This scripture tells us that we can either serve the Lord through our love for and obedience to Him, or serve mammon which specifically represents money and generally represents materialism and the things of this world. We cannot do both at the same time. We are given free will to choose, and choose we must.

1 John 1:7-9 states, "But if we walk in the light, as He is in the light, we have fellowship with one another, and the blood of Jesus Christ His Son cleanseth us from all sin. If we say that we have no sin, we deceive ourselves, and the truth is not in us. If we confess our sins, He is faithful and just to forgive us our sins, and to cleanse us from all unrighteousness." Please note, this scripture states, '*if*' we walk in His light, we are cleansed from all sin; and '*if*' we confess our sins, He will forgive us. Once our heart becomes hardened due to unrepentant sin, man typically no longer sees the need to ask

forgiveness and repent, and continues in that sin. By our behavior, we deny the Lordship of Jesus which puts us in a dangerous position of essentially returning to our original state prior to coming to Christ.

Isaiah 59:2 states, "But your iniquities have separated between you and your God, and your sins have hid His face from you, that He will not hear." This passage makes it clear that it was sin that separated God's people, Israel, from God. Throughout scripture, we see that this is true for all mankind. Sin still separates us from a holy God by degrading our fellowship with Him through walking in darkness! Hebrews 10:26, 29-30 states, "For if we sin willfully after that we have received knowledge of the truth, there remaineth no more sacrifice for sins. Of how much sorer punishment, suppose ye, shall he be thought worthy, who hath trodden under foot the Son of God, and hath counted the blood of the covenant, wherewith he was sanctified, an unholy thing, and hath done despite unto the Spirit of Grace? For we know Him that hath said, 'vengeance belongeth unto Me, I will recompense, saith the Lord. And again, the Lord shall judge His people."

This passage is referring to apostacy which, by definition, is a deliberate and known renouncement of one's once held faith. We can renounce our faith in heart, word, as well as deed. The result of apostacy is the act of intentional, deliberate, known continuation in sin after coming to Christ. And without faith in Christ Jesus, there are no other avenues to be reconciled back to God. Knowledge of this should compel a genuine believer in Christ to repent always before our Lord and King. When

21

we are forgiven by the Lord through faith in Jesus, we are spiritually cleansed.

Because we are imperfect beings, when we do inadvertently sin, we are to come before the Lord, confess our sin, humbly ask for forgiveness, and then repent. Repentance involves changing our heart attitude to reflect the heart attitude of the Lord which results in a change in our outward behavior. We ultimately stop participating in the sin of which we have repented. It is through this process that we demonstrate a real and living relationship with the Lord. Ongoing repentance should be our top priority. We should be ready *at all times* to meet our Lord and Savior. Please remember, the Lord judges us according to both our behavioral choices as well as the intentions of our heart. Only He is the perfect judge!

Conversely, *if* one believes in the doctrine of *once saved, always saved*, then it would not matter in terms of where we will spend eternity whether you remain obedient to God or knowingly, willingly continue to participate in unrepentant sin. Essentially, this doctrine taken to the extreme would be saying that sinning 'does not matter' as long as you 'just believe' because the grace of God 'covers us.' There are many self-professed Christians out there who believe this to be true. These Christians are Christian in word only, *not* in truth!

Jesus died a horrible death on the cross to *free* us from the bondages of sin and its wages of the second death which is eternal perdition. *Nowhere* in the bible does it state or even imply that Jesus' death on the cross allows us the freedom to willfully participate in continued, known sin with the reward of an eternity spent with the Lord. This heretical belief mocks and insults our Christ Jesus and makes what He did on the cross unnecessary and of no effect!

~

Ephesians 2:8-9 - For by grace you are saved through faith; and that not of yourselves: it is the gift of God: Not of works, lest any man should boast.

It is **only** by the grace of God that we are redeemed or saved once we come to faith and trust in Christ Jesus. It is a gift from God given to believers in Christ. Our good works done of the flesh cannot earn us salvation. However, it is important to note that once we are saved, we should and will execute good works of the Spirit which produces good fruit for the kingdom of God. James 2:17 states that faith without works is dead.

~

John 3:36 - He that believes on the Son has everlasting life: and he that believes not on the Son shall not see life; but the wrath of God abides on him.

This is just another of many scriptures that indicate that it is **only** by grace through faith in Christ Jesus that we are saved from eternal damnation and punishment, and results in eternal life spent with God. Again, we need to study all of the scriptures to understand if 'just believing' is 'all there is' to salvation, or if there is more to salvation than just belief. Again, consider the scripture that 'faith without works is dead.'

~

> *Romans 3:22-26 - Even the righteousness of God which is by faith of Jesus Christ unto all and upon all them that believe: for there is no difference: for all have sinned and fall short of the glory of God: Being justified freely by His grace through the redemption that is in Christ Jesus: Whom God sent forth to be the propitiation [appeasement] through faith in His blood, to declare His righteousness for the remission of sins that are past, through the forbearance of God; to declare, I say, at this time His righteousness: that He might be just, and the justifier of him which believes in Jesus.*

These beautiful verses of scripture tell us that salvation is available to *all* mankind: Jews and non-Jews alike! We cannot earn salvation through good deeds or good works. Prior to being saved, we are all inherently sinful in the eyes of God and fall short of His glory.

However, please note that above in Romans 3:22-26, it states that we have all *sinned*, which is in the past tense, meaning *prior* to our salvation by grace through faith in Christ Jesus. In no way do any of these scriptures imply that continuation in known sin is acceptable after we come to Christ! Remember, sin separates us from a holy God which is why we need to repent often!

Some proponents of the *once saved, always saved* doctrine believe that because the Gospel includes payment for sins we haven't even committed yet, that we can continue in sin after professing belief in Jesus and still enjoy the privilege of spending eternity in heaven with the Lord. What heresy! That is **not** what scripture states. Our sins are forgiven only when we have a repentant heart, confess our sin, and purpose to turn away from the sin!

Luke 13:3 states, "I tell you, Nay: but, except ye repent, ye shall all likewise perish." This was referring to some recent calamities where many people died. The people of Israel thought these victims died by calamity because they were unusually wicked. However, the Lord warned them that *unless they repent,* they would all likewise perish. Basically, this is stressing the importance of repentance to restoring and remaining in right standing with the Lord. Again,1 John 1:9 states, "If we confess our sins, He is faithful and just to forgive us our sins, and to cleanse us from all unrighteousness." Praise the Lord for His grace and long suffering for us!

God's only begotten Son, Jesus, willingly paid the price for **all** the sins of mankind on the cross. The penalty of sin is death. Jesus defeated sin and death on the cross through His shed blood and His resurrection from the dead. It is **only** by the grace of God through our faith in His Son, Christ Jesus, that we are saved from eternal damnation with the assurance of eternal life spent with Him.

The question we need to ask is whether or not this is the totality of the story of salvation or perhaps, just the starting point of salvation? We also need to ask if it is possible to lose your salvation if you choose to knowingly, intentionally reject Christ Jesus and the gospel message in the future after coming to faith in Jesus.

Luke 23:39-43 tells the story of the two thieves who were each hung on a cross on either side of Jesus. One of the thieves taunted Jesus, while the other thief rebuked the one who taunted Jesus saying, "Don't you fear God?" He continued saying that they were in fact guilty of a crime and deserved this punishment while Jesus was innocent of any wrongdoing. Then, he spoke to Jesus addressing Him as 'Lord' and asked to be remembered when Jesus came into His kingdom. In verse 43, Jesus replied, "Verily I say unto thee, today thou shalt be with Me in paradise."

The proponents of the *once saved, always saved* doctrine frequently utilize these verses of scripture to substantiate their claims. They believe that, based on these scriptures, **all** one has to do is believe in Jesus, and the One who sent Him, in order to be saved. Some proponents of this doctrine go on to say that 'all' we have to do is believe and say this out loud once and 'we are good to go!' Although this is somewhat true, it does not address the changes in our heart attitudes with resultant changes in behavior that will be demonstrated over time in the life of a true believer with saving faith. Faith without works is dead. (James 2:17). Our changed behavior and good works of the Spirit are the fruit, or evidence, of a changed heart and saving faith for those of us with more time to spend on this earth after our initial salvation experience.

I am certain that there have been and will be many unsaved, sinful people who sincerely confess Jesus as their Lord and Savior on their deathbed, who were forgiven by the Lord, and received salvation at the last minute, and went on to spend all eternity with the Lord. However, I am sure that these people absolutely must have had *truly* repentant hearts in order to be saved. Only God can correctly judge the heart of man. We do serve a loving and merciful God who would have it that none be lost, and who also happens to be a perfect judge. Praise the Lord for He is good!

The one thing the people in these illustrations of the thief on the cross and the deathbed 'convert' have in common is a last minute, sincere coming to the Lord with a truly repentant heart before they breathed their last breath. If they had more time to live on this earth, they would have had to have chosen to live their lives with the same directive that Jesus gave to the woman caught in the act of adultery in John chapter 8. He did not condemn her, but told her, "Go, and sin no more!" He also told the man He had healed at the pools of Bethesda in John chapter 5 to "sin no more, lest a worse thing happen to him." This certainly implies there may be more to salvation than just a mere belief and verbal profession of faith in Christ Jesus for those of us with more time to live upon the earth.

At this point, I would like to add that *if* you are purposing to live a life of self-indulgent sin in this world with the intention of professing Jesus as Lord and Savior on your deathbed so you can have a great eternity spent with Him; it is a very, very risky plan to say the least! Many carnal people feel that this would be a 'win-win' scenario where we can have unbridled sinful 'fun' on earth as well as enjoy a fabulous eternity with the Lord. This could not be further from the truth.

First of all, just saying these words of salvation is **not** a 'get out of hell free' card. You have to truly mean it in your heart. God knows and **will** correctly judge your heart. **Only** a truly repentant heart demonstrates real faith in the Gospel.

Secondly, no one is guaranteed tomorrow (Proverbs 27:1.) Any of us could suffer an unexpected and very quick death on this earth which affords zero time to truly repent. We must take this into consideration.

~

2 Corinthians 5:17 - Therefore, if any man be in Christ, he is a new creature: old things are passed away; behold, all things are become new.

He that is in Christ, or a genuine born-again Christian, has the Holy Spirit of the living God dwelling on the inside of him. He is no longer a child of Satan in bondage to sin, but is now a child of the living God who has been set free from the bondages of sin, and the wages of sin which is death. The primary focus of our heart and mind has changed from self and temporal things, to God and eternal things. This change of heart and change of focus ultimately changes our behavior. It is by our changed heart and changed behavior that we can know that we truly have become a new creature in Christ!

If someone is truly born-again and has the Holy Spirit living inside their heart, we will see positive changes in their heart attitudes, thinking and behavior. Most often, these changes occur over time.

However, what conclusions might we come to regarding

a person who said the prayer of salvation yet over time, just continued in their sin without any changes in their heart attitudes, thinking or behavior? One possible conclusion would be that they were never saved to begin with in this case. I am sure this is true in many instances. But is this the only possible conclusion? Another possibility is that they were once saved but walked away willingly by choice through free will which was never taken away. This person would be an apostate. But, there is yet another possible third conclusion.

The proponents of the *once saved, always saved* doctrine who believe that once you are saved, you can never, ever lose your salvation no matter what, also believe that the one who is saved yet continues a life of known, deliberate sin will always be heaven-bound but will lose or forfeit their eternal rewards or crowns. Let's take a scriptural look at this third opinion.

1 Corinthians 3:14-15 states, "If any man's work abide which he hath built thereupon, he shall receive a reward. If any man's work shall be burned, he shall suffer loss: but he himself shall be saved; yet so as by fire."

James 1:12 states, "Blessed is the man that endureth temptation: for when he is tried, he shall receive the crown of life, which the Lord hath promised to those who love Him."

Revelation 2:10 states, "In the last portion of verse 10 Jesus states: "be thou faithful unto death, and I will give thee a crown of life".

Revelation 3:11 states, [Jesus speaking] "Behold, I come quickly: hold that fast which thou hast, that no man take thy crown."

Matthew 6:5-6 states, "And when thou prayest, thou shalt not be as the hypocrites are: for they love to pray standing in the synagogues and in the corners of the streets, that they may be seen of men. Verily I say unto you, they have their reward. But thou, when thou prayest, enter into thy closet, and when thou hast shut thy door, pray to thy Father which is in secret; and thy Father which seeth in secret shall reward thee openly."

All of this is to say that, for those of us who are saved and heaven-bound, Christ will judge our works done while we lived upon the earth as well as judge the heart attitude by which we did these works. We were all appointed kingdom works to accomplish upon this earth by God before we were even born. (See Jeremiah 1:5; Ephesians 2:10.) We will receive rewards for those works done with a right heart attitude which bore good fruit for the kingdom of God. Conversely, we forfeit our rewards and suffer that loss for those times we failed to complete those kingdom works assigned to us or when we executed those assigned tasks with a wrong heart attitude. However, both still remain in eternity with the Lord because in both instances, the person described had a heart of love for, faith in, and obedience to the Lord such that their salvation remained secured. The difference is between hearing 'Welcome home! Well done My good and faithful servant' vs. 'Welcome home, you made it here by the skin of your teeth' (author's phrasing for effect) upon a saved person's arrival into heaven with the Lord. These scriptures only discuss the rewards or lack thereof for whether or not *faithful* believers completed their God ordained missions with a right heart attitude while living upon the earth. These scriptures in no way address the possibility and eternal result of falling away or apostacy.

Getting back to our original issue of the possibility falling away from the faith or apostacy, we need to remember that only God can correctly judge the heart of man. I bring this up not to specifically judge anyone, but to inquire if it is possible for someone to walk away willingly from the truth after they become saved. We also should seek to understand if it is possible to lose our salvation if we intentionally purpose to continue in known sin without repentance after being saved. The validity of the doctrine of *once saved, always saved in* ***all*** *circumstances* is what is in question.

~

1 Corinthians 10:13 - There hath no temptation taken you but such as is common to man: but God is faithful, who will not suffer (tolerate) you to be tempted above that ye are able; but will with the temptation also make a way to escape, that ye may be able to bear it.

This scripture is saying that God will provide enough strength for us to overcome any temptations with which we are presented in our lifetime through the power of His Holy Spirit who now resides in a genuine believer. God does His part to guide and protect us, but we have to do our part to resist the temptation and continue to walk in righteousness. This is basically saying that followers of Christ have no excuse for falling into or remaining in sin as God faithfully provides the means of escape to remain free from the bondages of sin and death once you are saved by grace through faith in Christ.

There are two points for consideration that I would like to make:

1. The Holy Spirit and the grace of God given to those who are saved gives us the power to overcome sin, *not* permission to continue in sin.

2. Holy Spirit filled people are in a partnership with God. We cannot do God's part, and God *will not* do our part. This does imply intentional *action* on our part after our initial profession of faith in Christ Jesus. This *action* is in the form of intentional obedience to the word of God. Galatians 5: 24 states, "And they that are Christ's have crucified the flesh along with the affections and lusts."

This leads me to my next question, which is: What happens, in terms of eternal destination, to the knowingly and intentionally disobedient unrepentant believer in Christ Jesus? The bible is clear that sin cannot enter heaven (1 Corinthians 6:9-10), and unrepentant sin is not forgiven. (1 John 1:9) However, some proponents of the *once saved, always saved* doctrine would conclude that they go to heaven, of course, because they believe that one cannot ever lose their salvation under any circumstances. Conversely, other proponents of this doctrine would claim that they would go to hell because they were never saved to begin with based on their unchanged behavior. I find these conclusions to be contradictory, not to mention convenient to the believers in the *once saved, always saved* doctrine.

Clearly, we need to dig deeper into what the word of God in the bible has to say about this! Certainly, nobody should 'hang their hat' on the opinions of others, including mine, concerning their eternal destination. The opinion of God is the only opinion that matters, and we must search His word in the bible to find it!

~

Romans 8:38-39 - For I am persuaded, that neither death, nor life, nor angels, nor principalities, nor powers, nor things present, nor things to come, nor height, nor depth, nor any other creature, shall be able to separate us from the love of God, which is in Christ Jesus our Lord.

What a beautiful scripture this is! It speaks of the immense love that God has for each and every one of us as His creation. Even though the sin of humanity in the garden of Eden separated us from our Creator, God sent His only begotten Son to the earth to pay the price for our sins so that each and every one of us could be reconciled back to Him. This is a golden *opportunity* given to each and every one of us as His beloved creation. We must choose to accept Jesus as our Lord and Savior while we are living on this earth in order to be reconciled back to God to partake in eternal life with Him.

God desires that His beloved creation would choose Him, but He will not force us to make any particular choice. There have been, are, and will be those that choose to reject Jesus and what He did on the cross for them. There have been, are, and will be those who don't even give their eternity or God a second thought. Sadly, no choice is a choice in terms of where one will spend eternity. Although God still loves each and every one of them as His creation, their eternity in hell separated from Him is set by the choice they made to reject or ignore Him while on earth.

As my late pastor husband would frequently say, "God will love you all the way to hell! It is the choices we make while on this earth that determine our eternal destination!" Because of God's undeniable great love for us as His creation, each and every one of us has the same opportunity to spend eternity in heaven with the Lord! Please, let that sink in. The choices we make upon this earth determine our eternal destination. Choose wisely!

~

1 John 3:9,24 - Whosoever is born of God doth not commit sin; for His seed remaineth in him: and he cannot sin, because he is born of God. And he that keepeth His commandments dwelleth in Him, and He in him. And hereby we know that He abideth in us, by the Spirit which He hath given us.

This scripture is referring to the fact that known, willful, and habitual sin simply is not demonstrated in a genuinely born-again Christian because the Holy Spirit within us will convict us of sin, which leads us to repentance. A born-again believer in Christ will have a heart that purposes to be intentionally obedient to the word and commandments of God, and this heart attitude

34

will be evident in their behavior. Just as the Lord gives people grace, we must also give grace and support to a sibling in Christ who is purposing in their heart to stop sinning but might still be struggling with their behavior over time to stop participating in their sin. This challenge is particularly true in new converts.

The proponents of the *once saved, always saved* doctrine utilize these scriptures to justify their beliefs by stating that no one who is **truly** saved will commit known, willful and habitual sin and, therefore, will never lose their salvation. Certainly, there is truth to this statement.

It is also true that the Holy Spirit gives believers the strength to overcome sin **if** the believer **chooses** to cooperate with His promptings. We must remember that, often times, this is a process that occurs over time and is driven by our heart attitudes. However, there is no biblical indication that once we are saved by grace through faith in Christ, our **ability to continue** to choose between good/God and evil/self is removed from us. It appears that our inherent ability to choose, our free will, remains throughout the duration of our lives here on earth. Once we are saved, we are invited into a partnership with God, not forced bondage.

Again, can a professed Christian lose their salvation if they choose to continue in known, habitual, intentional and unrepentant sin? This is an extremely important question to ask. Why?

For example, how many professed Christians, who go to church weekly and participate in regular church activities, also secretly participate in fornication, adultery, pornography, intentional deception, greed, love of power, and the like? Many believe that 'God will understand' because they are only human and not perfect. Additionally, some believe that a particular sin is no longer sin if society claims the behavior is acceptable and legal. If the *once saved, always saved* doctrine is false, saved people who purpose to continue in known sin will be the ones with weeping and gnashing of teeth when they unexpectedly hear these words from the Lord, "depart from me for I never knew you."

For those readers out there who love the Lord and are saved yet continue to struggle with sin, please remember that the Lord also considers the intentions and attitudes of your heart, and not just your behavior. Jeremiah 17:10 states, "I the Lord search the heart, I try the reins, even to give every man according to his ways, and according to the fruit of his doings." You must take a good, hard, prayerful look at the intentions of your heart. Are you purposing to stop sinning, or are you purposing to continue in your sin? Are you moving closer to the Lord, or further away from Him? Are you making progress over time in no longer participating in sin? When you backslide into your sin, does it grieve your heart? Honest answers to these questions will let you know where you are in your walk with the Lord. I urge you to take a good, hard, and honest look at the intentions of your heart as well as your behaviors. Your eternity is at stake!

Please remember, the bible is a book of victory, not a book of defeat! The Holy Spirit within us gives us the power to overcome sin in our lives!

~

> *John 10:27-30 - [Jesus speaking], "My sheep
> hear My voice, and I know them, and they follow
> Me: and I give unto them eternal life; and they
> shall never perish, neither shall any man pluck
> them out of My hand. My Father, which gave
> them Me, is greater than all; and no man is able
> to pluck them out of My Father's hand. I and My
> Father are one."*

The definition of the word 'pluck' is to remove abruptly, forcibly; to seize. In this instance, this scripture is saying that we cannot be *forcibly* removed from relationship with God against our will by an outside force. However, in no way does this scripture address the possibility of us *choosing* to walk away from God of our own free will. It only states this cannot happen against our will by an outside force.

God gives each and every one of us the free will to choose to follow Him or not, to choose between good and evil. When we make that decision and choose to follow Christ, invite Him into our heart to be our Lord and Savior, *and* follow Him for the remainder of our earthly life; only then will one be saved by the grace of God through faith in His only begotten Son, Christ Jesus, with the promise of eternal life spent with God.

What does it mean to follow Christ? When Jesus walked the earth, He led by example. We are to follow His example. Jesus always perfectly obeyed the Father in heaven as well as the word of God set forth in the Old Testament. This is the bar that Jesus has set for His followers here on the earth. Of course, as fallible human beings, we cannot follow the Lord perfectly as we are

37

inherently imperfect. However, the intention of our heart to serve and obey the Lord can be perfect as well as consistent if we so choose. If our heart is right before the Lord, when/if we do err and sin, the Holy Spirit convicts us of our wrongdoing, and we will feel remorse and be quick to repent.

~

> *John 3:5-6 - Jesus answered, "Verily, verily, I say unto thee, except a man be born of water and of the Spirit, he cannot enter into the kingdom of God. That which is born of flesh is flesh, and that which is born of Spirit is spirit."*

There is some controversy as to the meaning of 'born of water' in this scripture. Some believe it to be referring to water baptism, some believe it to mean the physical process of human birth because the baby is encased in a fluid/water sac, while others believe it to be a reference to Christians being 'bathed' in the Word of God. What I would say to this controversy is this:

1. Get water baptized as an adult if you are able to do so. It is our public declaration of our faith in Christ Jesus. Scripture says we are to confess Jesus with our mouth in Romans 10:9. Conversely, if we deny Jesus before man, He will deny us before the Father in heaven as per Matthew 10:33.

2. As human beings, we all have been born naturally surrounded by 'water.' This is just a given for every one of us, Christian or not.

3. If we profess to be a genuine born-again Christian; we will read, learn, and study the Word of God. Desiring to learn more about God and His Word should be an inherent drive in each and every born-again Christian.

It is very clear in the scriptures that we must be infilled with the Holy Spirit of the living God in order to be saved and have eternal life with the Lord. This is what it means to be 'born-again' or born of the Spirit.

~

John 6:39-40 - [Jesus speaking], "And this is the Father's will which hath sent Me, that of all which He hath given Me I should lose nothing, but should raise it up again on the last day. And this is the will of Him that sent Me, that every one which seeth the Son, and believeth on Him, may have everlasting life: and I will raise him up at the last day."

God's will is that none *might* be lost, and that every person who comes to faith in Christ Jesus would willingly choose to continue in their faith in Christ. Technically, just because God wills that all *may* be saved does not mean that He is indicating that everyone *will* be saved no matter what.

What John 6: 39-40 is saying is that everyone has the same *opportunity* to be saved by grace through faith in Christ Jesus. However, not everyone will choose this path. God *prefers* that everyone be saved, but He allows us the free will to choose our path in this life with its resultant eternal destiny.

The question that begs to be answered is can we still intentionally change our mind and walk away from our salvation through faith in Jesus Christ after we are saved? The bible refers to this as apostasy. Since apostasy is mentioned in the New Testament, it appears that this is certainly a possibility.

~

> *1 John 2:3-4,19 - And hereby we do know that we know Him, if we keep His commandments. He that saith, I know Him, and keepeth not His commandments, is a liar, and the truth is not in him. (19) They went out from us, but they were not of us; for if they had been of us, they would no doubt have continued with us: but they went out, that they might manifest that they were not all of us.*

There are many who believe in the doctrine of *once saved, always saved* who utilize 1 John 2:3-4 to go on to claim that those who leave the church or depart from the faith were never really saved to begin with. They reason that, if they were truly saved, they would have never left the faith and the church. I am sure that this claim is true in many instances. However, can we say without **any doubt** that this is true in **all** cases?

~

> *Ephesians 4:30 - And grieve not the Holy Spirit of God; whereby ye are sealed until the day of redemption.*

Many proponents of the *once saved, always saved* doctrine focus on the second half of this scripture which says, once we are filled with the Holy Spirit, we are sealed until the day of redemption. They feel it is a guarantee that we will spend eternity in heaven with the Lord after we say the prayer of salvation. However, if this is true, then why does the first half of this scripture give a warning for Spirit-filled believers to not grieve the Holy Spirit? If we are sealed in the Lord until our redemption, why would we even need to care if we grieve the Holy Spirit if we are already guaranteed our eternity in heaven?

We need to understand what it means to grieve the Holy Spirit. We grieve the Holy Spirit whenever we disobey God. The surrounding scriptures list the many behaviors that if a Spirit-filled believer did would sorely grieve the Holy Spirit. Some of these behaviors include fornication, adultery, covetousness, foul language, and the like. In other words, sin grieves the Holy Spirit.

~

Romans 11:29 - For the gifts and calling of God are without repentance.

This scripture is saying that God does not revoke his gifts and calling to His people even during times of rebuke and punishment. For example, both the Jews and the Gentiles have been disobedient to and have sinned before their God. According to scripture, God turned his offer of salvation to the Gentiles from the Jews because of the disobedience of the Jews. It is God's heart that the salvation of the Gentiles will lead to the salvation of the

Jews. God still loves His Israel! The Jews still have an open door to repentance and salvation should they so choose, just as do the non-Jews.

The main takeaway point is that the door to salvation remains open for all. It is God's desire that all would be saved. We are saved by the grace of God through faith in His only begotten Son, Christ Jesus. Once we have been saved, we demonstrate the genuineness of our salvation through obedience to God and His word. Again, the choices we make on this earth determine our eternal destination.

CHAPTER THREE

Bible Verses Which Invalidate the
***Once Saved, Always Saved* Doctrine:**

Matthew 7:21-23 - [Jesus speaking], "Not every-one that saith unto Me, Lord, Lord, shall enter into the kingdom of heaven; but he that doeth the will of my Father which is in heaven. Many will say to Me in that day, Lord, Lord, have we not prophesied in your name? and in thy name hath cast out devils? And in thy name done many wonderful works? And then I will profess unto them, I never knew you: depart from Me, ye that work iniquity."

I find these scriptures in Matthew to be very sobering. I cannot imagine anything more crushing than unexpectedly hearing those words from my Lord and Savior, Jesus.

In this passage, Jesus is referring to two different types of people. The first type of person is the one who only hears the word of God but does not follow or obey the word of God. Clearly, God expects obedience to His word from His true followers who will spend eternity with Him. John 14:15 states [Jesus speaking], "If ye love Me, keep my commandments." Our obedience to the Lord and His word is an outward sign of the love we have for Him. Disobedience, iniquity, and sin are all various forms of rebellion against God and will result in eternal separation from Him if there is no repentance. It really is that simple.

The second type of person is the one who may have preached in the name of Jesus and even done mighty works in the name of the Lord simply because there is power in the name of Jesus, but their hearts were far from Him. The Lord also accuses them of being workers of iniquity. The word 'work' implies an active act of intention, while 'iniquity' means wickedness. Therefore, although they may have performed miracles in the name of Jesus, the motivation and intention of their heart was steeped in wickedness. Such people will also spend eternity apart from the Lord in hell.

What we can gather from these scriptures is that our actual behavior, as well as the intentions of our heart, are what the Lord will base His judgment upon when we stand before Him. The bible clearly and repeatedly lists all the behaviors that the Lord considers sinful so that each one of us is given the opportunity to evaluate our behavior according to the Lord's measuring stick, so to speak, in His word. Again, our behavior is an outward manifestation and indication of our inner love for and faith in the Lord.

We can look at the parable of the sheep and the goats in Matthew 25:31-46 for further illustration. I would like to begin by stating that there are three main judgments yet to occur. One will be when Christ comes to judge all people on earth when He returns to reign for the millennium; another will be the Judgment seat of Christ which occurs after the rapture where He rewards believers for their works on earth; and the final white throne judgment where Christ will judge the wicked and consign them to an eternity in the lake of fire. The separation of the sheep from the goats is referring to the judgment of the nations when Christ rules over the earth.

The sheep represent those people who came to the Lord and were gentle and kind, and who were obedient to the Lord out of their love for the Lord. Their faith produced good works or fruit. They will spend eternity with the Lord. The goats represent those people who did not come to the Lord and were not gentle or kind, and were not obedient to Christ. Their faith or lack thereof produced bad fruit or nothing at all. The goats will be sentenced to an eternity in the lake of fire. All this is to say that a saving faith will produce good works, as faith without works is dead (James 2:24-26). Again, we are only saved by grace through faith in Christ Jesus, and our good works by the Spirit are the evidence of our saving faith.

Additionally, there are scriptures which clearly indicate to us the importance of searching our hearts frequently to ensure that they are truly and fully dedicated to the Lord and His kingdom purposes. We must ask the Lord to show us any areas of iniquity in our heart or our lives so that we may truly repent of them. These scriptures illustrate the importance of being obedient to the Lord, as well as having and maintaining a right heart attitude before the Lord to ensure an eternity spent with Him. For example, Hebrews 3:12 states, "Take heed, brethren, lest there be in any of you an evil heart of unbelief, in departing from the living God." Hebrews was written to the believing Jews and warned them it was in fact possible to depart from faith in Christ.

There are also scriptures which illustrate the possibility that we can be deceived about our salvation and eternal destination. The New Testament scriptures were written to believers, not unbelievers. As such, it is more probable that these passages refer to people who were professed believers, but their love of and faith in the Lord diminished over time, possibly unawares.

For example, in a paraphrase of Revelation 2:1-7, Jesus speaks to the church at Ephesus through His scribe, the apostle John. One of the issues Jesus chastises the Church at Ephesus for is that although their good works were plenty, they had lost the love they had for Him at first. I suspect that their initial deep love for the Lord was eventually replaced with a very strong adherence to religious rules and regulations. Perhaps, a spirit of disbelief also may have developed over time. Either way, their hearts were now far from Him even though on the surface it appeared they were still doing the work of God. Jesus tells them they need to repent of this, or He will remove their lampstand/candlestick from its place. Essentially, Jesus said that their hearts were in the right place at the beginning of their relationship with Him when they were first saved, but He found their heart attitude quite lacking now, and if they did not repent of this, they would be discarded from His presence. That is a very sobering message from the Lord which indicates that it is possible to lose one's right standing with the Lord if there is no repentance from sin, which would result in an eternity spent separated from Him. Furthermore, to the church of Sardis, the Lord promised the believers there who kept true to their Christian testimony that He would not blot their names out from the Book of Life, unlike those there who had returned to their prior worldliness. These words indicate that it is possible to have one's name blotted out of the Book of Life after it has been added. This is another very sobering passage in scripture.

John 14:21 states [Jesus speaking], "He that hath my commandments, and keepeth them, he it is that loveth Me: and he that loveth Me shall be loved of My Father, and I will love him, and will manifest Myself to him." Again, it is both our obedience as evidenced through our behavior, and the heart attitudes and motivations that accompany our behavior, that are extremely important to the Lord. If obedience and heart attitude is important to the Lord, it should be very important to His true followers also.

John 14:21 actually runs counter to the belief that all one has to do is say the *sinner's prayer* and they are saved and on their way to heaven no matter what. The *sinner's prayer* is one where someone confesses their belief with their mouth that Jesus Christ is the Son of God who took away their sins through His death on the cross, and their belief that God resurrected Him from the dead. We must believe this in our heart while we pray it. Truthfully, the *sinners' prayer* is not in the bible and was developed during the reformation in the 1500's around the same time that Calvin's *once saved, always saved* doctrine appeared on the theological scene.

This being said, John 14:21 indicates that this is not enough just to say these words in order to guarantee an eternity spent with God in paradise. We must also *do* the

47

will of the Father. This means that we are to be obedient to the word of God in the bible as well as to any individual directives He may give us out of our love for Him. It points to our resultant obedience to God once we receive God into our hearts. We must choose to work cooperatively with the work of the Holy Spirit within us in order to live a life in obedience to God. It's not about talking the talk. We must walk the talk in our daily lives.

I would like to interject a story from my own life and walk with the Lord. This incident occurred very early in my walk with the Lord shortly after I was water baptized as an adult. I was newly saved! At this point in time, I had just received my first bible as a gift but had not yet even started reading it. I placed my new bible on the coffee table. I had just invited my mother, who was a staunch Catholic at that time, over for dinner. Just prior to her arrival, I noticed my new bible on the coffee table. I decided to hide my bible on a high shelf in another room to avoid having to justify my new-found faith to her, as I knew her reaction would be confrontational. We had a lovely visit. After she left, I went to the high shelf to get my new bible. It was gone!! I searched all over the house for the next couple of days to no avail. I knew where I had put it, but it was no longer there. A few days later, as I was passing through that room with the high shelf, the Lord stopped me in my tracks and said to me, "Deny Me before man, and I will deny you before the Father!" essentially quoting His own words written in Matthew 10:33! I glanced over and saw my bible on that high shelf where I knew I had originally placed it! This experience shook me to my core. I went on my face before the Lord and repented, and promised never to deny Him again. In obedience to the Lord, I spoke with my mother about my new-found faith a few days later. Even though I was saved when this happened, the Lord clearly let me know that there were expectations of me in my walk with Him and that if they were not met, He would deny me before the Father, meaning my eternal destiny would be in perdition instead of with Him in heaven. Through that experience with the Lord, He taught me directly that *once saved, always saved* is not true. Please learn from my experience and grievous error!

Specific Biblical Exceptions to
Once Saved, Always Saved

There are several scriptures which indicate that in specific circumstances, *once saved, always saved* is not true.

Revelation 14:9-10 - And the third angel followed them, saying with a loud voice, if any man worship the beast and his image, and receive his mark in his forehead, or his hand, the same shall drink of the wine of the wrath of God, which is poured out without mixture into the cup of His indignation; and he shall be tormented with fire and brimstone in the presence of the holy angels, and in the presence of the Lamb:

This clearly denotes **anyone**, even if they have said a salvation prayer and consider themselves to be saved, who worships the beast and takes his mark will suffer eternal damnation apart from God in the lake of fire. This is one example of a sin that God will punish with

49

eternal damnation.

I have heard some people, who claim to be born-again and seemingly produce good fruit, say that they would take the mark of the beast in order to feed their children. They went on to say that God would 'understand,' and that they believed they would still spend eternity with God. Yes, God would 'understand' simply because He is an omniscient God who understands the deceitfulness of the human heart. His word clearly states that *anyone* who takes the mark of the beast and worships the beast will be condemned to eternity in fire and brimstone. His word is His word and cannot be denied!

Another scripture that creates an exception to *once saved, always saved* doctrine is:

> *Matthew 12:31 - [Jesus speaking], "Wherefore, I say unto you, all manner of sin and blasphemy shall be forgiven unto men: but the blasphemy against the Holy Ghost shall not be forgiven unto men."*

Blasphemy of the Holy Spirit involves defiant irreverence and rejection of the work of the Holy Spirit. In practical terms, it is ascribing evil to the work of the Holy Spirit and refusing to submit to the work of the Holy Spirit. For instance, the Pharisees ascribed the good work of the Holy Spirit done through Jesus to be of the devil. Jesus declared their willful blindness to be unpardonable. Blasphemy of the Holy Spirit is another sin that God clearly states will *never* be forgiven of anyone. This is true for anyone, both saved as well as unsaved. Apparently, there are now two exceptions to the doctrine of *once saved, always saved*.

A third scripture that creates an exception to *once saved, always saved* is:

Revelation 22:19 - And if any man shall take away from the words of the book of this prophecy, God shall take away his part out of the book of life, and out of the holy city, and from the things which are written in this book.

Interesting. God will take his part out of the Book of Life should *any* man take away any words from the book of Revelation. Think about this: one has to be saved in order to have one's name written in the Book of Life. And one has to be in the Book of Life in order to be removed from it!

We have just discovered three sins that will not be forgiven by God and those guilty will be spending eternity separated from God in damnation. Taking the mark of the beast, blasphemy of the Holy Spirit, and adding to or removing words from the book of Revelation will result in eternal perdition according to the word of God!

The Apostle Paul also makes clear that in the latter days, believers will depart or fall away from the faith.

1 Timothy 4:1 - Now the Spirit speaks expressly, that in the latter times some shall depart from the faith, giving heed to seducing spirits, and doctrines of devils:

This scripture clearly states that in the latter days, some shall depart from the faith. One has to have faith first in order to depart from it. We are saved by the grace of God through faith in Christ Jesus. Therefore, we must admit that falling away from the faith is possible according to scripture which means we can *choose* to reject God after being saved. Clearly, this would alter our eternal destination from being with the Lord to one of damnation.

Once we come to have faith, nowhere in the bible does it say we can never, ever change our mind and depart from the faith. This scripture actually says some shall depart or leave their faith in the latter days. God never takes away our free will to choose to love and obey Him or choose not to do so. It is His desire that all would choose to love and obey Him so that none would be lost, but nowhere in the bible does it say that God takes away our ability to choose after we make our initial choice. The fact that scripture states that falling away will happen in the latter days testifies to this.

Lastly, the Apostle Paul states in no uncertain terms that if we deny Jesus, He will also deny us, echoing the words of Jesus Himself.

> *2 Timothy 2:12b – "...if we deny (Him), He will also deny us"*

Remember, we can deny the Lord in heart, word, or deed. I take these passages of scripture very, very seriously, as I hope all of you will also!

Faith and Obedience: Examining and Working Out Our Salvation

> *James 2:14, 17-19 - "What doth it profit, my brethren, though a man may say he hath faith,*

and have not works? can faith save him? Even so faith, if it hath not works, is dead, being alone. Yea, a man may say, Thou hast faith, and I have works: shew me thy faith without thy works, and I will shew thee my faith by my works. Thou believest that there is one God; thou doest well: the devils also believe, and tremble."

Matthew 8:28-29 - "And when He was come to the other side into the country of Gergesenes, there met Him two possessed with devils, coming out of the tombs, exceeding fierce, that no man might pass by that way. And, behold, they cried out, saying, What have we to do with Thee, Jesus, thou Son of God? Art thou come hither to torment us before the time?"

These passages of scripture are very interesting in that they tell us that even the devils know and believe in the gospel that Jesus truly is the Son of God, just as human believers do. Yet, the eternal fate of the devils has already been set in the lake of fire, which is why they tremble.

My next question to you would be, if both devils and humans believe in and profess Christ Jesus and the gospel story, why would the eternal fate of the devils be any different from the human believers if believing is the only requirement to an eternity spent in heaven with the Lord? To say that the devils who believe will spend eternity in hell fire, while all believing humans will spend eternity in heaven, based on the argument that salvation is based on belief alone, does not make sense with the understanding that we serve a righteous God.

So, what is it that differentiates true, genuine, saved believers in God from demons who also believe in God and confess His Son? In Matthew 8:28-29, we can see through scripture that demons certainly know fully well who God is and confess that Jesus is the Son of God, yet they remain knowingly and intentionally disobedient to God! The devils hate God and hate what Jesus accomplished on the cross for us. Sadly, known and intentional disobedience to God can be true of human believers also. Why would we think that human beings who verbally state that they are saved and believe in the one true God while they live their lives in intentional, known, habitual, unrepentant disobedience to God have an eternity any different from demons?

What differentiates genuine believers is a deep love of God with resultant love for our fellow man. It is our belief and faith in the Son of God, coupled with a love for God and a love for everything He loves, that propels us to live in obedience to His teachings and to live a life of sacrificial service, or good works, towards others.

Jeremiah 17:9-10 states, "The heart is deceitful above all things, and desperately wicked: who can know it? I the Lord search the heart, I try the reins, even to give every man according to his ways, and according to the fruit of his doings." Clearly, the Lord judges our heart attitude along with its resultant works.

This being said, our good works and deeds are *not* what save us. We are only saved by the grace of God through faith in His only begotten Son, Christ Jesus. When we are filled with the Holy Spirit of the living God, our hearts are changed, which changes our minds, which changes our behavior. We now execute good works of the Spirit out of love for the Lord in cooperation with the promptings of the Holy Spirit, who now resides within us. When our hearts are right before God, obedience to the Lord and His teachings naturally follows salvation. Again, James 2:17 states plainly that faith without works is dead. This scripture implies that good works done through obedience to the promptings of the Holy Spirit is an expectation of the Lord once we have a saving faith, and are an outward sign that we belong to Christ Jesus. Again, these good works of the spirit do not save us, but are the good fruit produced from someone with a true and saving faith in the Lord.

Proverbs 4:23 states, "Keep thy heart with all diligence; for out of it are the issues of life." Our inner life resides in our heart and mind. Our heart attitudes form the basis of our thoughts, and our thoughts produce our actions and behaviors both good as well as bad. We must strive to guard our hearts!

Acts 21-22 states, "Thou hast neither part nor lot in this matter: for thy heart is not right in the sight of God. Repent therefore of this thy wickedness, and pray God, if perhaps the thought of thine heart be forgiven thee." True repentance, meaning turning away from sin, stems from feeling grieved in our heart when we are convicted of sin by the Holy Spirit. True repentance leads to our forgiveness when we humbly confess our sins to God with a contrite heart and ask this of God. Proverbs 28:13 states, "He that covereth his sins shall not prosper: but whoso confesseth and forsaketh them shall have mercy." We must admit our sin to God with a contrite heart and purpose to turn away from that sin in order to be forgiven and restored into right fellowship with God. Our need for ongoing repentance should never be taken lightly!

This said, because we are human beings who struggle against our flesh, it is a foregone conclusion that we will err and sin at times. This is because we are imperfect human beings and will continue to make mistakes, coupled with the fact that our flesh remains an enemy of the Spirit of God within us even after we are saved. This can be seen in Galatians 5:17 which states, "For the flesh lusteth against the Spirit, and the Spirit against the flesh: and these are contrary the one to the other: so that ye cannot do the things that ye would."

Human beings will not have perfect behavior at all times. However, we can have a right heart attitude of love for the Lord with a strong desire to be obedient to the Lord in all things at all times. This will make us quick to seek forgiveness and repent of sin in our lives as the Holy Spirit convicts us. Sometimes, the Lord delivers us immediately from a sin, and other times it is a process that occurs over time. When the repenting of a sin occurs over time, our Lord is longsuffering and patient with us to give us the time needed to overcome sin. It is His desire that none be lost (2 Peter 3:9.) The Lord is most gracious to look at our heart attitude during those times of challenge and struggle.

During these times of challenge when we have not fully repented of and overcome a particular sin, we need to ask ourselves what it is we really desire to do? Is it truly our heart's desire to move closer to the Lord and repent of the sin, or do we love the sin and hope that God will understand? Do we feel remorse when the Holy Spirit convicts us of sin? Your honest answers to these questions are indicative of where your heart truly is concerning the things of the Lord. Be honest with yourself because the Lord already knows the truth about you!

I cannot stress this enough. Believing humans are saved by the grace of God through faith in Christ Jesus. But this is only the *starting* point in our walk with the Lord. As our faith in and knowledge of God deepens, so should our walk with Him. This means our thoughts and our heart attitudes will become more and more like His, which results in our changed behavior. Our lives become more and more about pleasing and serving the Lord. We leave sin behind and press into our Lord. We will happily do the works of the Spirit as He leads. We are not saved by works, but our works of the Spirit are the result of our love for, obedience to, and relationship with the Lord. *If* we continue steadfastly in this, we will be heaven bound with the Lord for all eternity.

Matthew 24:13 states, [Jesus speaking], "But he that shall endure unto the end, the same shall be saved." Again, we must remain steadfast and true to our Lord and Savior, Jesus, until our very last breath on this earth. The opposite of remaining steadfast is falling away or apostacy, which results in a very different eternity.

Let's review the seed that landed on rocky soil in Luke 8:13. This describes the person who receives the gospel message with enthusiasm and accepts Christ Jesus as their Lord and Savior. Many in today's Christianity would claim that this person is now saved by grace through faith in Christ Jesus. And this is true. However, also according to this parable of Jesus, the roots did not grow deep and the plant withered away, meaning this person fell away from the faith when persecutions, tribulations, and challenges to their faith came along after having received the knowledge of the Lord. Again, scripture points to the fact that falling away is a possibility after coming to faith in Christ and receiving salvation. After our initial moment of salvation, our ability to choose to remain true to the Lord or later depart from the Lord remains.

The good news here is that a truly repentant heart is forgiven and remade into right standing with the Lord. We have free will to choose, and it is the choices we make here on earth based on our heart attitudes that determine our eternal destination. Unlike the devils whose eternal fate has already been determined, for us human beings, there is still hope for us as long as we are alive! We should be very grateful to the Lord for this!

~

John 14:15 - [Jesus speaking], "If you love me, keep My commandments".

Those who love Jesus will purpose to obey His comm-andments plus any specific directives He might give us individually. This scripture does not imply that obeying *most* of the commandments is sufficient. That would be akin to man's standards of saying 70% is passing and, therefore, satisfactory! Rather, a truly saved person will purpose to obey *all* of the Lord's commandments. We cannot cherry-pick those commandments with which we agree as being the ones we will obey, while ignoring and disobeying the commandments with which we disagree.

Any disobedience is sin. Our love of God should surpass our love of self and our love of sin. Anything we love or value more than God is an idol before Him, and idolatry is sin!

I would like to point out that God is the same yesterday, today, and forever as per Hebrews 13:8. This means that God's opinions and directives do not change over time. What God has deemed sinful remains sinful in His eyes forever, even if modern day society legalizes or condones a particular sinful behavior.

It is obvious from John 14:15 and Matthew 24:13 that after one professes faith in Christ Jesus, obedience to the Lord is an outward expression of our faith in Him and our following Him, a result of the love we have for Him, and the result of a heart that purposes to fully serve and obey the Lord. Being saved by grace through faith is only the beginning of our walk with and towards the Lord. Simply believing and confessing with our mouth is not all there is to being and remaining saved.

Nowhere does scripture claim that the *only* thing you have to do is profess your faith in Christ Jesus and His work on the cross in order to be saved with no further expectations from God. In other words, scripture does not say that *all* you must do to be saved is confess Christ once, and you are saved for all eternity without regard for how you choose to live your life forward after confessing Jesus as your Lord and Savior.

~

Hebrews 5:9 - ...and being made perfect, He became the author of eternal salvation unto all that obey Him;

Obedience to Christ after our initial profession of faith is vital to ensure our eternal salvation. After our initial conversion, there will be a change in our heart attitudes to become more and more like Christ. Our behaviors will noticeably change. Although these changes can be instant-aneous, they are more commonly seen to develop gradually over time.

Thankfully, the Lord gives us much grace and is very patient with us in order to give us time to fully repent. The Lord knows the intentions of our heart. The Lord knows when the focus of our heart is to be obedient to Him while we are struggling with our flesh to become and remain obedient to him in repenting of sin in our lives. God also knows if we are just giving Him lip service with the hidden intention of our heart being to continue on in our sin, hopefully unnoticed, because that is what we truly desire.

~

> *Philippians 2:12 - Wherefore, my beloved, as ye have always obeyed, not as in my presence only, but now much more in my absence, work out your own salvation with fear and trembling.*

In this passage, Paul is writing to fellow believers shortly before his anticipated martyrdom. We must ask why Paul would state that we even need to **work** out our own salvation if the doctrine of *once saved, always saved* in all instances were true? Remember, the doctrine of *once saved, always saved* was a concept introduced 1500 years after the death and resurrection of Christ Jesus, and was **not** a concept taught by the Apostle Paul, who had greater revelation of Jesus than just about anyone. This fact speaks volumes to me.

What does this mean to work out our own salvation with fear and trembling? It means we are to take the issue of whether or not we are saved very, very seriously. We must continually watch, pray to, seek, and depend on God to ensure we are truly saved and remain truly saved. Our level of steadfast obedience to Christ Jesus and the good fruit it produces is the only objective measure we have to assess our personal salvation without hearing directly from the Holy Spirit Himself, as I did in that bible hiding incident I shared earlier.

1 Samuel 16:7 states, "But the Lord said unto Samuel, Look not on his countenance, nor on the height of his stature; because I have refused him: for the Lord sees not as man sees, but the Lord looks upon the heart." This scripture should give all of us imperfect people who deeply love the Lord much hope!! We might not be able to have perfect performance all the time while we are on this earth because we are inherently imperfect, but we can have a perfect heart towards the Lord which includes a deep love for Him along with a yearning and intent to be obedient to Him in all things. When the struggle against sin is real in our lives, we need to remember that we do serve a merciful God whose grace to us is new every day!

~

2 Corinthians 13:5 - Examine yourselves, whether ye be in the faith; prove your own selves. Know ye not your own selves, how that Christ is in you. Except ye be reprobates.

61

Why would we even need to examine ourselves after we have been saved *if* the *once saved, always saved* doctrine is true? How do we test ourselves to be sure that we are truly saved? We need to read, study, and know the word of God in the Holy Bible, and compare ourselves to it in terms of our heart attitudes, desires, behaviors and lifestyle. Of course, this should be a continual process over the course of our physical life on earth. This is referred to as our 'walk' with the Lord after that moment in which we initially became saved. Again, salvation begins with our profession of faith in Christ Jesus, but it does not end there! There is a process of justification (the process of being made righteous before a holy God) and sanctification (being set apart for God's purposes) that needs to happen as we cooperate with the work of the Holy Spirit who now resides within us. Basically, we are to look and behave more and more like Jesus as we continue to grow in Him.

Galatians

> *Galatians 1:6 - I marvel that you are so soon removed from him that called you into the grace of Christ unto another gospel.*

In his letter to the Galatians, Paul was amazed that those to whom he taught the true gospel message and who embraced it fully, could later completely turn their backs to the true gospel and embrace a false doctrine. Again, this speaks to the possibility that a follower of Christ can later embrace a false doctrine, thus walking away from faith in the one true God through Christ Jesus, His Son.

It is akin to a seed that lands on rocks and sprouts short, weak roots, and soon withers away (Matthew 13:5-6.) How can we assume and say with total certainty that such a person who walks away from the faith was never saved to begin with as proponents of *once saved, always saved* would claim? We cannot say this because we cannot correctly judge the heart of man. Only God can correctly judge the heart of man. Again, it is safer to err on the side of caution since our eternity is at stake here!

In Matthew 13:20-21, the explanation of the scripture regarding the seed that lands upon the rocks is given by Jesus. To paraphrase, the seed that falls on rocky ground and sprouts up quickly represents the person who initially receives the gospel message with great joy. Remember, since we are saved by grace through faith in Christ, it certainly would appear that such a person is now saved. However, their joy and faith in the Lord is short lived because of shallow roots; aka a lack of discipleship, a laziness on their part to grow their initial faith, or a failure to rise above tribulation and persecution, all of which can result in a walking away from the faith. It again appears that walking away from the faith is possible according to scripture. However, since only God can know the true heart of man, all we can conclude from this scripture is **either** they were never saved to begin with, **or** they walked away from the faith. Only God is omniscient and knows the truth for such a person.

Galatians 5:17 - ...the flesh lusts against the Spirit, and the Spirit against the flesh: and these are contrary to one another.

Later in Paul's letter to the Galatians, he tells us that, once we are filled with the Holy Spirit, our flesh and our Spirit will be at war with each other. Our flesh-nature is inherently sinful. In order to overcome sin during the process of sanctification, we must purpose to act against our fleshly lusts while acting in agreement with the promptings of the Holy Spirit. This takes intention and action on our part, and although it may not be easy, the Holy Spirit does give us the power to ultimately overcome sin!

There may be times when we stumble in sin, but Spirit-filled believers will be quick to feel remorse and quick to repent once we feel the conviction of the Holy Spirit within us. This being said, with the understanding that our free will to choose is never taken away, we must ask: Is it possible that a saved person who follows Jesus can decide at some point that they no longer want to follow Jesus and instead, choose to follow their own fleshly lusts to the point of ultimately denying Him?

How could a person who knowingly and intentionally rejects or denies Jesus with whom they once had a relationship, but later returned to a life of self-serving sin, wind up in eternity in glory with the Lord while in that unrepentant state? If we choose ourselves and a life of sin over God, we are placing ourselves above God which is idolatry! Idolatry is a sin which denies that God is rightfully above all other gods!

Matthew 10:33 states, [Jesus speaking], "But whosoever shall deny Me before men, him will I also deny before My Father which is in heaven." We can deny God in our heart, with our words, and with our actions. There are negative eternal consequences for those who choose to knowingly and intentionally deny Christ.

Paul continues by listing specific acts which are of the flesh. Note that words in brackets were added by the author to define specific words Paul used in the scriptures.

> *Galatians 5:19-21 - Now the works of the flesh are manifest, which are these: adultery, fornication, unclean-ness, lasciviousness [lust], idolatry [something worshipped or valued above God], witchcraft [use of magic, worship of nature, evil], hatred, variance [inconsistencies ,differences, argumentative], emulations [imitation, attempts to surpass another], wrath [great anger with desire to punish], strife [bitter disagreement], seditions [to incite rebellion], heresies [contrary teachings], envyings [discontentment], murders, drunkenness, revelings [excessive partying], and such like: of which I tell you before, as I have told you in time past, that they which do such things shall not inherit the kingdom of God.*

It is very clear from these scriptures and others like it that people who practice sinful behaviors such as those listed previously will not spend eternity with God. By use of the word 'practice,' it is meant that such sinful behavior is planned out or done willingly, knowingly, and habitually. Nowhere does it state that these scriptures apply *only* to the unsaved. They clearly imply that *anyone*, saved or not, who practices these behaviors will not spend eternity with the Lord. Period.

Many people erroneously believe that after they say the

sinners prayer where they claim that they believe Jesus was the Son of God who died for their sins and rose from the dead, and also claim Christ Jesus as their Lord and Savior for the forgiveness of their sins, can now live a life any way they choose because they are forgiven and saved, and as such will spend eternity with God in heaven. These are those who use the doctrine of *once saved, always saved* as a license to sin here on earth with the belief that they will spend eternity in glory with the Lord regardless of the behavioral choices made and heart attitudes developed here on the earth. This could not be further from the truth, as many scriptures indicate in the Word of God. This is the greatest danger to those who choose to believe in this doctrine.

Some believers in the *once saved, always saved* doctrine will say that, *if* a person is *truly* saved and filled with the Holy Spirit, they will not continue in a life of sin. If they do continue in a life of sin, they reason that the person was not *truly* saved and filled with the Holy Spirit to begin with. I certainly do agree that this *may* be true in many instances, but I hesitate to believe and say that it is true in *every* case because humans cannot accurately judge the heart of another man. Only God can accurately judge the heart of man as He is the perfect judge. (See Proverbs 16:2, 21:2; Jeremiah 17:9-10.)

Therefore, we must conclude that known, intentional, unrepentant, continued participation in the above listed sins with resultant eternal perdition applies to *everyone*. These scriptures do not differentiate believers from unbelievers, and furthermore were originally written to believers!

Some proponents of the *once saved, always saved* doctrine assume one of two things when faced with a person who commits intentional, repetitive, unrepentant sin knowingly. The first assumption is that any person who participates in the aforementioned sins was never saved to begin with, therefore spending eternity in perdition where they belong according to scripture. Since humans cannot know the heart of a man, we cannot claim this with 100% certainty in all such cases. The second assumption is to erroneously conclude that a believer will never be punished and lose their salvation for purposing in their heart to commit unrepentant, known, habitual sin after their initial salvation experience. This is preposterous and contradicts the character of God and the purpose of the Gospel!

Jesus Christ died a horrific death on the cross to provide the way for man to be reconciled back to God, and to *free* us from the bondages of sin and death should we so choose. Jesus did not knowingly and willingly suffer on the cross as He did so that we could continue to wallow in our sinful muck and still receive the reward of an eternity spent with Him. If sin were 'ok' in the eyes of God, there would have been no need for Christ to go to the cross on our behalf.

We must believe that free will to choose between good/God and evil/self/the world remains after we are saved. God has expectations of those who choose to follow Him. Salvation is not about a moment in time following saying the sinner's prayer. Salvation becomes a narrow path upon which we must intentionally travel with Jesus. This process is called sanctification. But what happens if we become saved, begin the sanctification process over time, but at a future point in time knowingly and intentionally fall away from the faith and return to our prior sin without repentance? Will such a person still spend eternity with God?

The Apostle Paul also says something relevant about living by the spirit or by the flesh in his letter to the Romans.

> *Romans 8:13 - For if you live after the flesh, you shall die: but if you through the Spirit do mortify the deeds of the body, you shall live.*

This scripture does not delineate between the saved and the unsaved which indicates it applies to **all** people. Moreover, it was written to believers! It clearly indicates how the choices we make on earth, which are driven by our heart attitudes, determine our eternal destination. Nowhere does this imply that a professing Christian will continue to be saved after willfully, knowingly, and repeatedly purposing to disregard the Holy Spirit and live by the flesh in blatant disobedience to God without repentance! Such a heart attitude and behavior displays a disregard for and denial of the Lordship of Christ Jesus. This is apostasy!

But there is good news! Please remember it is the Holy Spirit within us that gives us the power to mortify or kill the deeds of the flesh and overcome sin! (See Romans 8:13.) Praise the Lord for His wonderful Holy Spirit!

Romans 2

> *Romans 2:4 - Or despise thou the riches of His*

*goodness and forbearance and longsuffering;
not knowing that the goodness of the Lord leads
thee to repentance?*

This scripture speaks about God's love and patience for
His creation. However, the purpose of God's love and
patience is to prompt us to repent. Repentance from sin
is an expectation of a follower of Christ. It was the
primary message that Jesus proclaimed. Praise the Lord
for His grace and patience with us, and His forgiveness
to the truly repentant!

*Romans 2:5 - But after thy hardness and
impenitent heart treasures up unto thyself wrath
against the day of wrath and revelation of the
righteous judgement of God;*

This scripture goes on to say that the heart that does not
repent stores up wrath for itself on the day of judgment
of the Lord. The Lord will repay each person according
to their works, good or bad. The Lord never takes away
our ability to choose. Again, unrepentance leads to
God's wrath, while repentance leads to forgiveness and
eternal fellowship with the Lord for each and every one
of us. It really is that simple.

*Romans 2:6-11 - [God] Who will render to every
man according to his deeds: To them who by
patient continuance in well doing seek for glory
and honor and immortality, eternal life: but unto
them that are contentious, and do not obey the
truth, but obey unrighteousness, indignation, and
wrath, Tribulation and anguish, upon every soul
of man that does evil, of the Jew first, and also of*

the Gentile; But glory, and honor, and peace, to every man that works good, of the Jew first, and also to the Gentile; for there is no respect of persons with God.

Paul goes on to speak to the importance of ***continuing*** in the faith as well as obedience to God after being saved for the assurance of eternal life with the Lord after our natural death on this earth. It also speaks of eternal damnation for those who knowingly and intentionally choose to follow unrighteousness and disobedience to God. These verses do not delineate between the saved and the unsaved in this matter. Therefore, these words apply to each and every one of us.

The Book of Hebrews

The Book of Hebrews was written to Jewish believers in Jesus. These Jews had believed on Jesus, but suffered much persecution for so many years that they were tempted to reject Jesus and return to the traditional Jewish faith and customs. However, since the death and resurrection of Jesus followed by the infilling of the Holy Spirit established a new covenant between God and His people, choosing to return to the old covenant would have meant falling away from the salvation God had made available through Christ. Therefore, those Jews that later knowingly rejected Jesus had no avenue for repentance and reconciliation back to God. Because of this, *if* they rejected the new covenant which was now in place, they could not be restored back into fellowship with God..

*Hebrews 3:12-14 - Take heed, brethren, lest there be any of you an evil heart of unbelief, in departing from the living God. But exhort one another daily, while it is called today; lest any of you be hardened through the deceitfulness of sin. For we are made partakers of Christ, **if** we hold the beginning of our confidence steadfast unto the end;*

Hebrews 3: 12-14 is specifically speaking about the Israelites during their wandering in the desert after their exodus from Egypt. As you may recall, it took the Israelites 40 years to arrive at the promised land in Canaan when the journey should have been completed in eleven days. Why did it take them so long to get there? After the Israelites witnessed the many miracles of God, including their deliverance from captivity in Egypt as well as their physical survival in the desert, their most grievous sin was their unbelief that their God was powerful enough to overcome the giants who occupied their promised land! Their unbelief angered God who then punished the Israelites. Their punishment was wandering in the desert for forty years, such that all but two of the original people who were twenty years of age or above at the time of leaving Egypt died in the desert and were not allowed to enter into the promised land and rest of God. Only Caleb and Joshua were allowed to enter the promised land and rest of God because they remained steadfast and true to the God of Abraham, Isaac, and Jacob.

What can we learn from this and apply to our lives today? One thing that screams out at me is the importance of maintaining a steadfast faith in the Lord in order to enter

His rest. Those who demonstrated unbelief through their actions of rebellion against God were rejected by God and not allowed to enter into His promise. Verse14 states the obvious that we must *maintain* the confidence we had in Christ at the beginning of our walk with Him all the way to the end of our lives in order to partake in eternal life with the Lord. Again, after we accept Him as Lord and Savior, we must continue in Him as part of the salvation process, thus making the doctrine of *once saved, always saved, regardless of future beliefs and behaviors,* simply not true.

It is crystal clear to me that we are daily given a choice to make regarding following the Lord verses fulfilling the lusts of our flesh thus denying His Lordship. It is our heart attitude along with the resultant daily choices we make that reveals what we truly believe about Him, and what we believe ultimately impacts our eternal destination. Our ability to make that choice is never taken away from us while we live upon this earth. The Lord's offer of eternal life with Him is *available* to everyone, but *only* those who make the choice to consistently love, follow, and obey Christ Jesus will experience eternal life with the Lord.

> *Hebrews 6:4-6 - For it is impossible for those who were once enlightened, and have tasted the heavenly gift, and were partakers of the Holy Ghost, and have tasted the good word of God, and the powers of the world to come, if they shall fall away, to renew them again unto repentance; seeing they crucify themselves the Son of God afresh, and put Him to an open shame.*

When we look at this scripture in terms of those of us living today, it illustrates plainly that it is possible for a Spirit-filled believer to fall away from the faith and reject it. This is called apostasy, which is a full renunciation of the faith, done intentionally and knowingly. The definition of apostasy is an abandonment or renunciation of one's religious (or political) beliefs. Note that one has to believe in something first, before they can renounce it.

Apostasy is different from backsliding. Backsliding is a sinful mistake that was not intentionally planned out and is genuinely regretted. Someone who backslides and genuinely repents is forgiven and restored into the faith. The apostate refuses to repent because their heart has been hardened as a result of willful continuation in known sin, and they are no better than the crowds who beat, tortured, crucified, and killed Jesus. The apostate will face the final judgment of God where there will be weeping and gnashing of teeth.

The fact that the New Testament speaks of and warns against apostasy clearly indicates that it is possible to intentionally and knowingly leave the faith and lose or throw away one's salvation.

Hebrews 10:26 - For if we sin willfully after that we have received knowledge of the truth, there remains no more sacrifice for sins.

This refers to the willful and intentional apostate. If a born-again believer knowingly, willfully, and intentionally renounces his faith in Christ and the gospel message and chooses to remain in known sin with no feelings of remorse or shame, there remains no more sacrifice for this person's sins. This person will suffer the same eternal consequence as the non-believers in perdition separated from God. Again, this scripture makes it very clear that there is no redemption for the willful, unrepentant apostate!

I would like to reiterate that the backslider has a different situation altogether from the apostate. The backslider may fall back into sin, but they do *not* renounce their faith in Christ and the gospel message, and their heart still loves the Lord *and* desires to be obedient to the Lord. A backslider will typically feel shame or remorse for their sin. There is still hope for their redemption *if* they repent.

If one continues willfully in known sin rather than repent after knowing the truth, there will come a point where the heart will become hardened and will no longer feel any remorse or shame in such behavior. God then turns his back on the one who has turned their back on Him. This is one reason why it is so vital that Christians are advised to repent so as to ensure our hearts do not become hardened. Repentance and obedience to the Lord becomes extremely difficult, almost impossible, for the one whose heart has become hardened due to sin.

> *Proverbs 29:1 - He, that being often reproved hardens his neck, shall suddenly be destroyed, and that without remedy.*

This confirms the previous scripture and conclusion. The Lord will graciously provide conviction and correction with longsuffering patience to our disobedience when we are filled with His Holy Spirit and have a heart for the Lord. This is to prompt us to repent! However, if we choose to willfully, intentionally, and knowingly continue in sin after we have been corrected and convicted, our hearts will eventually become hardened to the Lord. If we harden our hearts to the point that we deny Jesus as Lord, then the Lord turns us over to our reprobate mind. Without repentance, even one who was once a believer will die in their sin and suffer the same fate as the unbeliever!

Hebrews 10:29-31 - Of how much sorer punishment, suppose ye, shall he be thought worthy, who has trodden under foot the Son of God, and has counted the blood of the covenant, wherewith he was sanctified, an unholy thing, and has done despite unto the Spirit of grace. For we know Him that has said, vengeance belongs to Me, I will recompense, says the Lord. And again, the Lord shall judge His people. It is a fearful thing to fall into the hands of the living God.

This scripture refers to the severe punishment due to a person who was once saved and in relationship with God, who later treats the Lord with contempt and considers the shed blood of Christ Jesus to be of no effect and thus, blasphemes the Holy Spirit. God will show no mercy or forgiveness to such a person on the day of judgment.

This scripture also clearly denotes that a Spirit-filled Christian has the ability to walk away from God and renounce Him should they so choose! *If* that is their choice, they will suffer God's wrath. This scripture alone illustrates the doctrine of *once saved, always saved* regardless of our future heart attitudes and behavioral choices does not apply.

1 Corinthians 10

1 Corinthians 10:11-12 - [Author's note: the scriptures leading up to this point are referring to the Israelites behavior while they were in the wilderness.] Now all these things happened unto them for ensamples: and they are written for our admonition, upon whom the ends of the world are come. Wherefore let him that thinks he stands take heed lest he fall.

Quote from Clark's Commentary: "Let him who most confidently stands - him who has the fullest conviction in his own conscience that his heart is right with God - and that his mind is right in the truth, take heed lest he fall from his faith, and from the state of holiness in which the grace of God has placed him."

When we think about the Jews in the Old Testament, we can see that they believed that they were righteous and bound for eternal life with God due to their physical lineage or genealogy as God's chosen people. Fast forward a bit to the time of the exodus. The Israelites continued in their belief that due to their physical lineage, they were and would always be God's chosen people. I am sure they were exceedingly confident in this belief, perhaps even to the point of being prideful. But what happened during their time in the wilderness? They became angry with God and dissatisfied with His provisions, and turned to idolatry and rebellion against their God. Eventually, they demonstrated their unbelief in the power of God to make good on His word to deliver to them their promised land. As previously discussed, the punishment for their lack of faith and unbelief was that all but two of them who were over the age of twenty at the time of their release from Egypt died in the desert and did not enter into the promises and rest of God. It is very plain to see that God expects unwavering faith and obedience from His people. We are to learn from the mistakes of those who have gone before us.

The application for us today is that this scripture teaches us that followers of Christ need to take heed because falling away from the faith *is* possible. As Spirit-filled followers of Christ Jesus, we will live a life dependent upon our heavenly Father for direction and correction. We will pray and worship God in Spirit and truth, study His word in the Holy Bible, remain obedient to the Lord's teachings and personal directives, and fellowship with other Spirit-filled believers. Obedience is rewarded while unrepentant disobedience is punished.

Jesus said that anyone claiming to be a disciple of His, must pick up their cross and follow Him. (Matthew 16:24-26.) Should a follower of Christ stop taking up their cross, they will undoubtedly develop a change of heart towards the Lord. If they do this long enough without repenting, this person runs the risk of developing a hardened heart where backsliding can morph into apostacy which results in falling completely away from the Lord. I pray that no one reading this book is in such a state at that moment you come face to face with God. Each and every one of us will stand before Him and give account for ourselves after our earthly lives are done.

2 Peter

Peter wrote this letter as his final encouragement to believers so that they would persevere in the faith until the coming of the Lord.

> *2 Peter 1:8-11 - For if these things be in you, and abound, they make you that ye shall neither be barren nor unfruitful in the knowledge of our Lord Jesus Christ. But he that lacks these things is blind, and cannot see afar off, and hath forgotten that he was purged from his old sins. Wherefore the rather, brethren, give diligence to make your calling and election sure: for if you do these things, you shall never fall. For so an entrance shall be ministered unto you abundantly into the everlasting kingdom of our Lord and Savior Jesus Christ.*

These scriptures in 2 Peter remind us to remain diligent in all aspects of our faith in and walk with Christ Jesus. Why are we to remain diligent? We are to remain diligent to avoid the possibility of falling away from the faith in apostasy after having the full knowledge thereof. In our walk with Christ, we are either moving closer to the Lord or further away from the Lord. Those who do not remain diligent in all aspects of their newfound faith will eventually forget that they were cleansed of their sins when they came to Christ, and run the risk of becoming blind to the things of Christ once again. It is our growing faith in and love for the Lord once we are saved, along with our focus on eternity, that propels us to become and remain obedient to Christ and produce good fruit for the kingdom of God.

2 Peter 2:20-22 - For if after they have escaped the pollutions of the world through the knowledge of the Lord and Savior Jesus Christ, they are again entangled therein, and overcome, the latter end is worse with them than the beginning. For it had been better for them not to have known the way of righteousness, than, after they have known it, to turn from the holy commandment delivered unto them. But it is happened unto them according to the true proverb, the dog is returned to his own vomit again; and the sow that was washed to her wallowing mire.

First and foremost, this scripture refers to those who knew Christ through salvation and later willingly, intentionally, and knowingly rejected Christ and returned to their previous life of sin. That alone illustrates that our free will to choose is not taken away once we are saved. These scriptures indicate that it is, in fact, possible to lose one's salvation through the choices we make and the heart attitudes with which we make those choices.

These scriptures are saying that the state of a person who has been saved, but knowingly purposes to return to their life of sin *and* is overcome by it, is much worse off than their state of being in sin prior to being saved and having knowledge of the Lord. After having been spiritually cleansed through their faith in Christ, but later rejected this cleansing and returned to their prior filth or sin knowingly and willfully, the resultant eternal punishment for this type of known, intentional, willful unrepentant rejection of the truth will be eternal separation from God. Let that sink in!

Let's consider the plight of the fallen angels that are also referred to in Peter's writing. At one point in time, these angels walked with, talked with, lived with, and served the almighty living God. Certainly, we can agree that they all had knowledge of the truth and majesty of God. However, for reasons that we will not get into in this book, some of the angels willfully, intentionally, and knowingly purposed to rebel and sin against God. These angels were then cast out from God's presence. The eternal fate of these angels who rebelled has already been set by the living God. They will spend eternity in the lake of fire separated from God. (See Isaiah 14:12-21; Ezekiel 28:12-19; and Revelation 20:10.) Since we serve a perfect, righteous God who will ultimately judge everyone, why would we think that those humans who knowingly, intentionally, and willingly reject Christ Jesus without repentance after being saved would not have to suffer the same fate of the angels who knowingly, intentionally, and willfully sinned against God? Scripture is clear that God shows no partiality and does not have double standards.

> *2 Peter 3:17 - You therefore, beloved, seeing you know these things before, beware lest you also, being led away with the error of the wicked, fall from your own steadfastness.*

Again, this scripture warns us that it is possible to be led away from a steadfast faith in Christ Jesus through following a false teacher either knowingly or unknowingly. This is one reason why it is so important to know the word of God by reading and studying the word of God in the bible for yourself! The scriptures are very clear as to what the Lord God considers to be sinful and evil.

A false teacher will come to erroneous conclusions by taking scripture out of context to justify sin or justify their personal agenda. Sadly, there are many people who seek out these false teachers to justify their own sin while erroneously believing they are saved and heaven-bound. Again, the possibility of falling away from good standing with God through deception *is* possible according to scripture.

Enduring to the End to Receive Salvation

Matthew 24:13 - But he that shall endure unto the end, the same shall be saved.

"Endure *what* in order to be saved?" you might ask. Once we are saved by the grace of God through our faith in Christ Jesus, our walking the talk in obedience to God will cost us in this earthly life. We will suffer rejection and possible persecution to varying degrees. Some may experience rejection from their non-believing friends and family members. Some may face ridicule for their newfound faith. Some may even be martyred as many of our brethren have been and continue to be in some countries. This scripture tells us that those who *remain* true to their faith until the end of their lives on earth (or until the end of this world as we know it) will be saved and spend eternity with Christ Jesus. We must *choose* to remain true and steadfast to the Lord even during those challenging times in life so that we do not fall away from the faith due to fear, inconvenience, discomfort, or even death.

~

> *Romans 11:19-22 - Thou wilt say then, the branches were broken off, that I might be grafted in. Well; because of unbelief they were broken off, and thou stands by faith. Be not high minded, but fear; For if God spared not the natural branches, take heed lest He also spare not thee. Behold therefore the goodness and severity of God: on them which fell, severity; but towards thee, goodness,* **if you continue** *in His goodness: otherwise you also will be cut off.*

When one considers a large tree, it has a main trunk with many branches sprouting off of the main trunk. The main trunk represents God. The many branches growing off of the main trunk represent the people of God. The natural branches, representing the Jewish people, were cut off in God's judgment because of their unbelief in His Son, Jesus. It is because of this that the gospel message was then presented to Gentiles, or non-Jewish people. The Gentiles who believed in Christ Jesus were graciously grafted into the trunk, or into God's family.

These verses warn those very same Gentiles who were grafted into God's family through their belief in Christ Jesus (a.k.a. the Gentiles who are now saved by grace through faith) to **not** become over-confident in their salvation but to fear (respect) the Lord instead. Why? Because if they fall into unbelief as the Jews once did, the Lord would also cut off their branch in judgment because God shows no partiality.

These scriptures warn us of the vital importance of

continuing in steadfast faith in order to *remain* righteous before God and part of His eternal family. Again, this speaks of the possibility that a professing believer can, in fact, fall away from the faith. The Lord in His abundant mercy gives us many warnings in His holy word because it is His desire that none be lost.

~

Hebrews 3:14 - For we are made partakers of Christ, if we hold the beginning of our confidence steadfast unto the end;

We can see from this scripture that our steadfast, heart-based faith in Christ Jesus, coupled with our obedience to His teachings *until the end* is what guarantees us an eternity spent with the Lord. "To the end of *what?*" you might ask. The end of our natural lives on this earth, or the end of this world, whichever comes first. Acceptance of Christ Jesus as Lord and Savior by grace through faith is the starting point of salvation and the beginning of our walk with Christ. After our profession of faith, we *must persevere* in the faith with obedience to His teachings until the end in order to obtain an eternity with the Lord.

Salvation can be viewed as a two-part process: initial faith (justification) followed by maintaining our faith through the ongoing processes of sanctification. The fact that we must continue to maintain or hold onto our salvation through faith in and obedience to Christ once we are initially saved indicates the possibility that losing our salvation exists, thus negating the doctrine of *once saved, always saved.*

~

> *Colossians 1:21-23 - And you, that were sometime alienated and enemies in your own mind by wicked works, yet now has he reconciled in the body of his flesh through death, to present you holy and unblameable and unreprovable in his sight: IF you continue in the faith grounded and settled, and be not moved away from the hope of the gospel, which you have heard, and which was preached to every creature which is under heaven; whereof I Paul am made a minister;*

These scriptures say it beautifully and confirm the aforementioned scriptures and conclusions. The fact that many scriptures warn us of the ***need*** to grow in the faith and grow in obedience to the Lord indicates the possibility of falling away if we do not do these things after we become saved. This scripture specifically warns us to take heed so as ***not to be moved away*** from our hope in the gospel message. Praise the Lord for His provision and leading the way that leads us back to God!

Please note that Spirit-filled believers ***grow*** in our faith and obedience to the Lord over time. As fallible human beings, we will make mistakes and sin from time to time. However, when our hearts are right with the Lord, we will respond to the conviction of the Holy Spirit with remorse and a renewed desire and intent to not commit that sin again. During these times of challenge, God most graciously looks at our heart attitudes.

Think of it this way: we are either planning and purposing in our heart and mind to be obedient to the Lord and drawing closer to Him, or we are moving away from the Lord as our heart and mind purposes to knowingly and intentionally re-commit that same sin or a new sin repeatedly over time without repentance. We are taking a very serious risk with the Lord in terms of His judgment and our eternal destination if we continually place our flesh and our sin above God and His decrees.

~

Luke 8:13 - [A portion of the parable of the sower], They on the rock are they, which, when they hear, receive the word with joy; and these have no root, which for a while believe, and in time of temptation fall away.

In this particular parable, Jesus likens preaching the gospel message to a farmer planting a seed. The message is good, and the seed is good. However, in order for the seed to grow and produce good fruit, the soil in which it was planted must be fertile. Likewise, the gospel message or good word is planted into a person's heart and can only grow in a tender and receptive heart.

This portion of the parable presents a person who joyfully accepts and believes the gospel message for only a limited period of time. Today, many who joyfully accept and believe the gospel message will very soon afterwards say the *sinners prayer* and ask Jesus into their heart to be Lord and Savior. It is at this point that many are considered to be saved, and heaven-bound.

But reread the last portion of this scripture. It refers to a person who falls away from their newfound faith due to temptation. It certainly addresses the possibility of being able to change one's mind and heart and walk away from any faith in Christ Jesus. The bible is clear on the eternal destination of such a person who rejects Christ and the gospel message without repentance. The following scripture further confirms this conclusion.

> *Ezekiel 18:24 - But when the righteous turn away from his righteousness, and commits iniquity, and does according to all the abominations that the wicked man does, shall he live? All his righteousness that he has done shall not be mentioned: in his trespass that he has trespassed, and in his sin that he has sinned, in them he shall die.*

In this passage, Ezekiel is referring to God's justice and fairness that each will be judged for their own behavior and conduct, and that people have the capacity to change their mind, heart, and behavior even after being righteous at one point in time. If that person later knowingly and purposefully returns to their wicked and sinful life without any repentance, not only will his past time of righteousness not be remembered, but he will die in his sin and will suffer the eternal consequences thereof, which is an eternity separated from God in the pits of hell.

Though this scripture is from the Old Testament, it shows us that God is able to alter His judgment based on a change in a person's belief of heart and changed behavior. Therefore, it is my conclusion that it plainly and clearly runs counter to the *once saved, always saved* doctrine. In a new covenant interpretation, it speaks of those who once followed Christ and lived righteously, but had a change of heart with resultant change in behavior. In other words, they turned away from Christ only to intentionally, knowingly, and willingly return to a sinful lifestyle, away from following the Lord. It is possible for a born-again Christian to knowingly and purposefully turn away from and reject God without repentance, and to remain eternally separated from the Lord in hell. Please let that sink in!

~

Luke 9:62 - And Jesus said unto him, "No man, having put his hand to the plough, and looking back, is fit for the kingdom of God."

This scripture has a two-fold meaning, both literal and spiritual. In the example of a farmer plowing a field, if he were to continue plowing while looking behind himself, we can all agree that the furrow lines would no longer be straight, and the result would be a mess.

In another sense, if a follower of Christ were to look behind and focus on worldly treasures, he would not be able to move forward un-incumbered to spread the gospel message and serve the Lord effectively and whole heartedly. In both instances, the farmer and the follower of Christ have a strong interest on what was left behind. This will negatively impact their productivity in what lies ahead because their focus is divided.

Jesus' point in Luke 9:62 is that anyone who is following and serving Him while continuing to focus on or participate in activities of the world after being convicted by the Holy Spirit is not fit for the kingdom of God. God wants *all* our heart and soul and deserves nothing less. We need to prayerfully search our heart often to be sure it is right before God and be quick to repent of anything that the Lord finds displeasing.

The point here is that God has clear expectations of his followers. Anything less than meeting His expectations means we are not fit for the kingdom of God, again indicating that *once saved, always saved* in all circumstances is simply not true.

Consider also the parable of the ten virgins in Matthew chapter 25. In this parable, **all** of the virgins were betrothed to their bridegroom and expecting his return for them at any time. Only five of the virgins kept their full focus on the bridegroom and kept the oil in their lamps full with extra oil on hand just in case it was needed. The other five virgins did not keep their full focus on the bridegroom, and the oil in their lamps ran out before the bridegroom arrived. When the bridegroom arrived, **only** the five wise virgins who kept their full focus on him were allowed into the wedding feast. In Matthew 25:12, the bridegroom turned to the five slothful virgins and said, "Verily I say unto you, I know you not."

In the next verse Jesus states, "Watch therefore, for ye know neither the day nor the hour wherein the Son of man cometh." (Matthew 25:13.) If the doctrine of *once saved, always saved* were true in all instances and our eternity with the Lord assured once we say the *sinners prayer* and accept Christ into our heart, why would followers of Christ have to "watch and be ready" for the Lord's return? We could do whatever we want whenever we want, and just be pleasantly surprised when the Lord calls us home. Scripture proves over and over again that it does *not* work this way!

Revelation 3:5

I would like to end this chapter with a most sobering scripture:

> *Revelation 3:5 - [The Lord's letter to the church at Sardis] He that overcomes, the same shall be clothed in white raiment; and I will not blot out his name out of the book of life, but I will confess his name before my Father, and before His angels.*

Please note that it is the one whose purpose of heart and mind is to overcome the flesh and sin that Jesus will confess as His before the Father. The only way to overcome the flesh and sin is to be filled with the Holy Spirit, or saved, *and* to work in cooperation with the promptings of the Holy Spirit within us. Prompt repentance is key when we fail, as we will often do, in these imperfect earthly vessels.

But please, please make note of this: Jesus states that *only* those who overcome will *not* have their names blotted out from the Book of Life. Jesus is clearly letting us know that *it is possible* when we have an unrepentant heart and mind to continue intentionally in known sin and disobedience to Him to have our names blotted out of the Book of Life!

When we are saved, our names are written in the Book of Life. It is understood that the Book of Life only has the names of those who are heaven-bound to be with the

Lord for all eternity written in it. Consider this: our name has to be written into the Book of Life in order for it to be removed from the Book of Life. This scripture is saying that *it is possible* to lose one's salvation, with resultant change in one's eternity from being with the Lord to one of perdition separated from the Lord *if* one does not continue in the faith.

It is my position that believing in the *once saved, always saved* doctrine encourages us to take our guard down and just continue on in our lives without any further consideration about the things of God. As we have just read, this is contrary to several scriptures in the Holy Bible, and doing so will have a negative impact on our eternal destination

Chapter Four

Conclusion

In the beginning, according to the Book of Genesis, man walked and talked with God in the Garden of Eden. Man was created in God's image not only to give God glory and to do work for the kingdom of God, but to seek Him and be in voluntary fellowship with Him out of our love for Him. God instructed Adam that he could eat freely of any tree in the garden except the tree of the knowledge of good and evil. We all know the story: Adam and Eve disobeyed God and sinned when they ate from the one tree from which God told them not to.

Adam and Eve died spiritually in that day they sinned, and thus their sin separated them from God. Adam and Eve were then cast out of the Garden of Eden which began the process of man's eventual physical death as man no longer had access to the fruit of the tree of life.

On that day of their sin, Adam and Eve's eyes were opened to their physical nakedness, which represented their spiritual sin and spiritual death. Thankfully, God had foreknowledge of all of this, such that He already had a plan in place for the redemption of sinful man in that the lamb was slain before the foundation of the world. (Revelation 13:8.) Following that initial sin of man, God began the process of covering over sin. God made coverings for Adam and Eve's physical nakedness out of animal skin before he cast them out of the garden. Fast forward as we look into Jewish customs and practices through the years, all of this set in motion the practice of the annual sacrifice of an unblemished lamb in the temple to cover the sins of the Jewish people. This needed to be done once every year on the Day of Atonement or Yom Kippur! This was the way for sins to be forgiven in the old covenant, and was also a foreshadow of what was to come.

Ultimately, there needed to be a final, perfect sacrifice in order to provide the only 'once and for all' forgiveness of the sin of man. That perfect sacrificial 'lamb' needed to be a perfect man. Since there is no such thing as a perfect man, only God enrobed in flesh in the form of Christ Jesus could be that ultimate perfect and final sacrifice. Jesus greatly suffered and went to the cross knowingly and intentionally to be that final and perfect sacrifice not only for the forgiveness of sin, but to *free* everyone who believes in Him from the bondages of sin and death!

This gift from God is available to each and every one of us! However, we must make the choice to follow Christ in order to partake in this gift of righteousness, that is, right standing with God by grace through faith in Jesus. We must verbally claim Christ Jesus as our Lord and Savior and accept the truth of the gospel message. Yes, *if* we believe this in our heart *and* confess it with our mouth, we are then saved by the grace of God through our professed faith in His Son, Jesus. Praise the Lord for His most gracious and undeserved gift of salvation! But what are we to do with this most precious gift of salvation after we receive it?

The issue is that the scriptures also indicate that this

initial belief is only the ***beginning*** of our relationship and walk with the Lord. While it is true that nobody can forcefully take us away from Jesus against our will, scripture makes it very clear that we can either intentionally throw our salvation away or fall away from the faith if we are not careful. Scripture also indicates that it is our responsibility to grow our faith and deepen our newly restored relationship with the Lord God.

Once we believe in Jesus, how do we grow our faith and deepen our relationship with God? We do this by reading and studying the bible daily for ourselves so that we have knowledge of the truth in order to not be deceived. We need to fellowship with other born-again believers in Christ through church attendance and Christian-based social gatherings. We need to praise and worship our Lord in private as well as corporately. We need to spend time daily in prayer with the Lord. Finally, we need to ask the Lord in prayer to show us any areas of sin or poor heart attitude so we can truly repent of them.

Please understand that repentance is so much more than an empty apology. Repentance involves a humble admission of our sin to the Lord followed by a deep heart-felt remorse for any sin in our lives. This prompts a change in our heart attitude so that it is more in alignment with the Lord's heart attitude. Finally, this change in our heart results in a change in our behavior such that we will ultimately no longer participate in or practice that sin.

Since we are fallible and imperfect human beings, we will err and sin at times. But the Holy Spirit will convict us of sin and enable us to fully repent. Our gracious Lord truly does have our backs covered and gives us every opportunity to repent because it is His desire that none be lost! We truly do serve a loving and most gracious God!

I would like to, again, speak about apostasy which is mentioned several times in scripture. Apostasy is defined as a renunciation or abandonment of a religious belief. One has to have had faith and belief in something in order to renounce it, thereby making an intentional walking away from the faith *possible* according to scripture. One *can* throw away and lose one's salvation!

Finally, there are three instances of sin denoted in scripture where God has clearly stated that the end result of these sins will be an eternity spent in fire and brimstone. Only with blasphemy of the Holy Spirit does the Lord specifically state in scripture that there will be *no forgiveness*! This applies both to the saved and the unsaved as it applies to everyone. The three sins that result in eternal separation from the Lord in perdition are:

1. Blasphemy of the Holy Spirit (Matthew 12:31-32),
2. Taking the mark of the beast with worship of the beast (Rev 14:9-11), and
3. Taking away or adding to the Book of Revelation (Rev 22:18-19).

This fact alone that there exists three sins which result in eternal separation from a Holy God, and one sin that the Lord Himself specifically states that He will never forgive, makes the doctrine of *once saved, always saved* untrue. The fact that the scriptures repeatedly speak about falling away and apostasy indicates that it is possible to lose one's right standing, or salvation, with the Lord.

I like to think of salvation as a life-long journey rather than a moment in time. At that moment we confess Jesus as our Lord and Savior, we are taken off that wide path that leads to our destruction and are placed at the beginning of that narrow path that leads to a wonderful eternity spent with God. Once we are placed on that narrow path, we *must* work cooperatively and in obedience to the word of God and the promptings of the Holy Spirit who now dwells within us. It is only when we *continue* in obedient faith that we will reach the end of that narrow path which leads to an eternal life with the Lord. We are in a voluntary partnership with our God, never forced bondage. Our free will to choose is never taken away.

If the Lord has used this book to bring conviction to your heart about wrong beliefs, presumption, carelessness about sin, or sinful behaviors in your life that you need to repent of, please take it seriously. Put this book down and run to the presence of the Lord. Pour your heart out to Him and receive His forgiveness and mercy. Then, let your new way of believing start you on a new way of living and walking with Him until He calls you home or until He returns.

I hope to meet all of you one day in a wonderful eternity spent in the presence of our Lord and Savior, Christ Jesus! May the Lord bless and keep each and every one of you until that glorious time. Amen.

ABOUT THE AUTHOR

For as long as she can remember, Catherine Vitetta always loved her Lord and Savior, Jesus. Catherine and her husband, George, had a home church with multiple small community outreaches until George went to be with the Lord in 2022. Now, she is going even deeper in her relationship with the Lord by serving Him in new and unexpected ways, including writing books! It is her desire that this book brings clarity and sheds light on the doctrine of *once saved, always saved*, so that everyone can endure to the end and receive the fullness of our salvation!

About Manifest Publications

Manifest Publications is the publishing division of Manifest International, LLC. Our objective is to help like-minded ministries and writers produce and distribute materials which proclaim Jesus Christ to all the world and equip the global Church for unity and maturity.

MANIFEST
PUBLICATIONS

www.manifestinternational.com

www.ingramcontent.com/pod-product-compliance
Lightning Source LLC
La Vergne TN
LVHW021407080426
835508LV00020B/2484